Saving our World: Plan B

The Citizens' Mandate for Change and **You**

John Seymour

Published by Citizens' Mandate Ltd
Website: citizensmandate.com

ISBN: 978-1-3999-7724-1

First Edition

"To all those who are creating a better world."

Contents

Preface

The combined crises of climate change, environmental breakdown, and financial inequality are the biggest we have ever faced. We are looking at the collapse of global civilisation within perhaps 10 or 20 years. That's the bad news.

And the good news? Collapse is not yet inevitable. These crises are caused by our economic and political systems. If we change our systems, we can emerge from the crises transformed for the better. It could even be the biggest cultural renaissance of all time, and lead to a veritable golden age.

The problem is that we are locked into our present systems and the doom loop they create. It is repeatedly said that we lack the political will to make the changes we need to make, but there are few practical ideas for how we achieve this mythical 'political will'. Nor is there much well-developed thinking on the kind of systems we would need to replace our present ones with.

This book is ambitious and tackles these major issues head-on. The invention of the Citizens' Mandate for Change gives us all a political voice, which in turn creates the political will for change. And this political voice can emerge and grow from nothing more than talking with your friends and writing down what you think.

After looking at the threats we face in depth, most of the book explores the kind of changes we will need in our economic and political systems, and how these can come about in practice.

There's also a chapter helping to clarify each of our individual pathways through the times of change which lie ahead. The psychology of developing our emotional resilience allows us to thrive in times of stress.

The pages that follow lay all this out, and more. Above all, this book is a message of hope, and it maps out what may become our path of greatest hope.

For together *we can* change the world.

And we must.

Introduction

We live in difficult times with crises abounding. However, times of crisis are times of opportunity. Individually we may seem powerless, and yet there *is* something we can each do to bring about the changes most of us want. The Citizens' Mandate for Change, a social and political innovation, and a different kind of 'direct voting', gives us a shared political voice in a meaningful way for the first time. It involves your own answers to the three central questions of change: from what, to what, and how specifically? On the Citizens' Mandate itself they become:

What are the main issues you are concerned about?
What kind of society would you prefer to be living in?
What changes do you want our government to make?

The questions are simple, but not easy. First, clarify your answers by talking with friends and family. This helps you to get clearer, and it helps to spread the idea. Then go to the website: **citizensmandate.com** where four short videos explain the idea, and where you can cast your Mandate. If we can each interest at least three friends in doing the same within three weeks, and they do the same, that's all it takes. Our Mandate for Change will grow exponentially.

With the results summarised, the Citizens' Mandate for Change gives us a new kind of political voice. If it is an idea whose time has come, it will spread and can change everything. I believe little else can. This book maps a pathway forward and a message of hope.

My professional background is in change. Specifically, the precise changes that are necessary and sufficient to solve complex problems in organisations. Over some four decades, I've worked with hundreds of organisations and thousands of individuals who taught me much.

When I retired a few years ago, I began to ponder climate change as a problem; a particularly hard one, of course! I was drawn to writing a book about it. I enjoy reading, so I started to read about the subject in a more focussed way. In the last year alone, I've read over 120 of the most recent books by leading thinkers and writers in the field.

Some patterns began to emerge. Most books have much to say on the problems, and rather less on the solutions, but I wanted to write more about the solutions than the problems. Most books tend to come at it from a specialised viewpoint, however, I wanted to cover multiple viewpoints. Most had something useful to offer, but none a synthesis of all the most useful bits. So that, too, became a part of the task.

As if that wasn't enough, there was a big question hanging over it all. Was the task do-able? Was there a resolution, a pathway through? I simply didn't know. The problem looks 'wicked' in the sense of being so complex that it is not, in principle, soluble. It also looks to be intractable because the world's political and economic systems are strongly 'locked in' to the present state and are very resistant to change. Certainly no effective solution seems to have shown up so far. We are still on track for a climate catastrophe which will likely bring the end of civilisation as we know it.

Published in 2023 is a Synthesis Report from the Intergovernmental Panel on Climate Change which is a final warning and makes grim reading. Here is a quote from Antonio Guterres, the Secretary General of the United Nations:

"The climate time-bomb is ticking. But today's IPCC report is a how-to guide to defuse the climate time-bomb. It is a survival guide for humanity. As it shows, the 1.5-degree limit is achievable. But it will take a quantum leap in climate action. This report is a clarion call to massively fast-track climate efforts by every country and every sector and on every timeframe. In short, our world needs climate action on all fronts – everything, everywhere, all at once."

And so the quest to find a potential solution began. It felt like piecing together the bits of an outrageously complex jigsaw puzzle with no picture as a guide. It became clear that climate change cannot be viewed in isolation because everything is interconnected. Climate change is an unintended consequence of the economic systems, and the economic systems are determined by the workings of the political systems. Even though we live in a democracy, the workings of the political systems are dominated by vested interests and depend on our tacit consent and our relative powerlessness as individuals.

Overall, I became increasingly aware that these human-made complex systems are carrying us along a pathway which leads, apparently inexorably, to the collapse of civilisation. And yet there are still good reasons for hope; collapse is not inevitable and there is still time to turn things around, even at this late stage.

And central to that hope is the fact that we do have power as individuals. We each have a voice, including young people, and we can use it to great effect. And that is the purpose of the Citizens' Mandate for Change, central to this book: to use our individual voices to create a better world for all before we become too deeply embroiled in the beginnings of collapse, or the great unravelling, as some have called it.

On my journey, there were two significant breakthroughs. The first was eventually coming up with this intervention, the Citizens' Mandate for Change, a social and political innovation that potentially has the power to change things. It is made of your answers to just three questions, the most central questions of change.

By completing your Mandate and spreading it to friends, it has the potential to grow exponentially. This is how the Citizens' Mandate can become effective at massive scale. The website, **citizensmandate.com**, combines all the individual Citizens' Mandates into a summary of 'the voice of the people'. In retrospect, it seemed like the realisation of the obvious.

The second breakthrough was during our sixth take of the video clips for the website. Under the pressure of live performance, a short version of a coherent story emerged of how the Mandate can trigger transformational change.

Again, the story was obvious in retrospect, but I couldn't see it before.

After making that recording, I set to and wrote the first draft of this book. The whole thing seemed too urgent to wait for a traditional publisher. I wanted to launch the website and book together to support each other. Self-published it would have to be.

Once that was done, the experiment would be launched. The rest is down to how it is received, and the response it creates. I have done my best to make it plausible, credible, and compelling.

If you share the concerns of the majority about where we are heading, the Citizens' Mandate gives you a new option for taking action. Up until now, each of us has only had two main options. I haven't included voting here, as voting for one party or another once in five years is about as little choice as you could have.

Your two main options have been to either do what is within your power to reduce your own environmental damage, or to join the growing number of movements for change worldwide.

In Paul Hawken's book *Blessed Unrest* (2008), he estimated that there were then at least one million organisations working for positive change, and one in five people worldwide.

My estimate is that we now have some two million organisations for change and considerably more than one in five people working for change worldwide. Despite these impressive numbers, it has not yet been sufficient to change our tragic trajectory.

This third option, the Citizens' Mandate, if it spreads, gives us a new and different pathway to achieving the desperately needed changes so many of us want. Clearly, it will only spread if enough people participate. The purpose of this book is to spell out how exactly this third option may work in practice. Here is a brief overview of what we'll be looking at in each chapter.

Chapter One
Are We Doomed?

This chapter is about the human predicament and the threats we face.

We begin by looking not just at climate change, but at all the main threats we face. This enables us to see the climate crisis in the bigger context of all the other crises. It does, however, make for a rather uncomfortable read! If you are already feeling overwhelmed by the threats, I do not recommend starting here.

Begin instead with Chapter Two, which is where the path of greatest hope begins. Or, if you wish to boost your personal resilience, go straight to Chapter Ten which outlines some ways of coping with the threats on the personal level.

There's another reason why you may not want to start with Chapter One. If you have read what can seem like 'the doom literature', and are up to speed with all the threats, then begin on

Chapter Two. For everyone else, I will simply quote the writer and civic rights activist, James Baldwin, who put it like this:

"Not everything that we face can be changed, but nothing can be changed until it is faced."

Chapter Two
What Are the Fundamental Causes?

The climate crisis, like most of our other threats, is a symptom, but fixing the symptoms does not address the underlying causes. This chapter traces the levels of causation down to the fundamental ones by repeatedly asking 'why' questions.

So, for example, why are we having a climate crisis? Because we are producing too much carbon dioxide. Why are we producing too much carbon dioxide? Because we are burning too much fossil fuel. Why are we burning too much fossil fuel? Because the present economic system treats the environmental consequences of using fossil fuels as an 'externality'; that is, they are something outside the economic system. And so on.

Then we look at why we have such an unfit for purpose economic system. This leads to the political system which creates and maintains the rules of the game for the economic system. Why do we have such a dysfunctional political system? The multiple causes of this are explored in the last part of the chapter. Having mapped out the main fundamental causes, this leads on to…

Chapter Three
What Can We Do? The Citizens' Mandate

Here, I look at what each of us can do when faced with the dire state of the world. There are all the personal actions we can take such as flying less, eating less meat and so on. It all helps, but will never change the nature of our 'unfit for purpose' systems. And we can join some of the movements for change globally. That helps too, but hasn't yet changed our systems to make them fit for purpose.

Something else is needed, but what? It is often said that we lack the political will to make the changes we need. If we, the people, had a collective voice, would that be enough to empower political will? Could it actually change things? I believe it could. This chapter explores the Citizens' Mandate for Change which is on the website at **citizensmandate.com**. It has the three questions for your answers:

What are the main issues you are concerned about?
What kind of society would you prefer to be living in?
What changes do you want our government to make?

The website also has a few short video clips, podcasts, and texts which outline the whole project, as well as a free sample of this book. It has summaries of the Citizens' Mandate results and a planned online community. You can see how the project is developing with newsletter updates. And of course, you can send the link on to interested friends. Here, I look at the thinking behind the Mandate: what it is in detail, and how it can work in practice. I explore the notion of how, if it is the right idea, at the right time, it spreads rapidly and establishes a new norm. But of course, this only happens if enough people take it up, talk about it, and put it into action.

It is for you to decide if the Mandate is a good idea, or not. If you do, then you can discuss it with others, and act on it. And if they like it as well, they will do the same. If this happens, the rate of spread feeds on itself, just like compound interest. This is how we get to exponential growth.

Finally, the new idea reaches a threshold, a tipping point, where it becomes the new normal. Only then do governments act on it, just as they did with the anti-slavery movement, or votes for women. This tipping point is around 25% of the population.

So, 25% is the target of the Citizens' Mandate for Change. To reach 25% of the population, you need only reach 25% of your friends. In fact, reaching just three people in three weeks, who each do the same, is enough to do the job. If successful, the Citizens' Mandate can trigger a transformation in our systems, from the old ones which have had their day, to the new ones we need to deliver wellbeing for people and wellbeing for our global ecosystems before it is too late. Put simply, this project has the capacity to change the world! And little else does. This seems remarkable...

All of this is within your control. It doesn't cost money. All it takes is conversations with those of your friends who're interested. An attractive idea. But will it be compelling enough for you to act?

Chapter Four
Changing the Political System

In this chapter we explore what this might look like in practice, with the focus on the United Kingdom (UK). Clearly it would look a bit different in other countries, especially if they are not even notionally democracies. For example, what might the effect be in China? Would they embrace it or try to ban it?

If the Citizens' Mandate hits exponential growth and that magical figure of 25% before the next election, how might it change the dynamics of the election? What new coalitions, or new parties could emerge? What new ways of thinking and what new policies would become possible?

Of course, no one can predict what will emerge, not least because we don't know what views will show up in the Mandate itself. But we can predict that it will have a massive impact on the status quo. Therefore, much of this chapter is of necessity speculative in nature.

It explores some of the changes we may see in our somewhat antiquated democracy. It also looks at some of the leading-edge practices in other democracies. This includes a few of the different forms of massive online democratic processes from participatory budgeting to 'liquid democracy', and to Taiwan's online democratisation of governance itself.

We look, too, at some of the best thinking on how to redesign parliament, so that it can become fit for purpose. And finally, we explore the emerging Green New Deal (GND).

Chapter Five
Governance Systems for a World Which Works

If it is true that our major problems are caused primarily by the unintended consequences of human-made systems, then the main causes of our problems are systemic, i.e. relating to our systems. And if they are systemic, then the many branches of systems thinking may offer a useful way forward.

Cybernetics, the study of organisation in complex systems, was the beginning of all the different forms of systems thinking we now have. In this chapter we explore one particular systems-thinking model in some depth. This model lays out what is necessary and sufficient for any complex system to be able to continually organise and maintain itself in the face of the complexity of the real world. It lays out the guiding principles of what works best in practice.

Called the Viable Systems Model (VSM), it was developed by Stafford Beer in the seventies based on how living systems organise themselves, and applied most famously in Chile by President Allende. Sadly, it was cut short by a military coup. But it did begin the process

9

of discovering how to make governance more effective and exploring how to do it in practice.

Another fertile source of innovation, much under-used, is deceptively simple. This is to look for the best practice examples from around the world and replicate the key elements of what makes them work. You don't keep trying to reinvent wheels!

When we look at the governance of other countries, one country that keeps coming up as one of the top performers by many measures is Finland. We explore what exactly the Finns do differently to other countries that leads to their outstanding levels of both performance and wellbeing.

Lastly, we take a long hard look at the forces that prevent us from moving in these positive directions. It will come as no surprise to you that this takes us to the vested interests, those who benefit massively from the way things currently are.

Perhaps slightly less obvious is the role that the established media play in this. With few exceptions, the print media are owned by billionaires, a tiny fraction of the 1% of the wealthiest, and we'll look at how they exert their stranglehold on the way in which we perceive the world.

The billionaire-owned press is where the fightback will come from; and it will be fierce. We look at the likely stages of this fight as they would apply to the Citizens' Mandate movement. The press will probably begin with ignoring the Mandate, moving on to ridiculing it, and then to attacking it extremely aggressively, and eventually there comes the final stage in which we win, and a new normal becomes the established reality. Of course, if we fail to establish a new normal in the world of politics, business-as-usual wins, and we all face social and ecological collapse.

Chapter Six
Changing Our Economic Systems

The way our present economic system works is the underlying cause of most of the major problems we face, from the climate crisis to ever-increasing financial inequality. Economics is a murky area, and most people's eyes glaze over at the mere mention of it. Yet we need a basic understanding of how the economic system works, or rather doesn't work, if we are to improve on it.

First, we take a quick look at the present system, called neoliberal economics, which has ruled the roost for the last 40 or so years, and the main ways in which it is dysfunctional and not fit for purpose. We also look at how it is fundamentally different to Keynesian economics, which dominated the 30 years after the Second World War, and gave much better social outcomes; this was the so-called golden age of capitalism.

Clearly, neoliberal economics needs to be replaced with a different economic system. What are the best options? We take a quick tour of some of the most promising ones. First up is Kate Raworth's Doughnut Economics model which outlines the main aims of maintaining a safe operating space for humanity within the framework of the safe environmental planetary boundaries.

After this, we explore steady-state economics, the circular economy, and low material growth systems. We also look at some of the changes we will need to make to taxation in the fiscal system, the system in which governments raise and spend taxes.

The monetary system, on the other hand, is the system by which governments create the supply of money which keeps the whole economy running. We'll look at some of some of the best thinking on the kind of changes we will need to make to the monetary system. This includes Modern Monetary Theory (MMT) and Mariana

Mazzucato's explorations of the role of the new kind of entrepreneurial state we will need.

On then to the part business can play in the coming transformation: the present 'for profit' shareholder corporation, and the up-and-coming stakeholder corporations with benefits spread more broadly.

Next is a more speculative exploration of the coming generation of business structures which are likely to emerge and the kind of measures they will use. The notion of carbon productivity is introduced, the ability to produce more of real value with the use of less carbon dioxide. Also we consider the related notion of social productivity, the ability to produce more of real social value with lower social costs. Then there is an outline of the different measures of social inequality that we use.

The chapter finishes by looking at how we can pull our best economic options together with a proposal of the kind of changes that we need, and which are do-able. It also flags up the need for an overarching transition plan of around ten years to guide us from the system we are currently stuck in, to the new and self-evolving systems that a better future demands of us.

Chapter Seven
The Green New Deal and Earth for All

In this chapter we take a closer look at two of the main contenders for integrating all of the above into a coherent program for change which could work politically.

There is a wide range of Green New Deals. Some seem to me to be relatively superficial in that they don't get to the heart of the underlying systemic causes of our problems. I've chosen the British

Green New Deal (BGND) because, in my opinion, it goes further in this direction than most.

The BGND is built around seven main principles:

- A steady-state economy
- Limited needs, not limitless wants
- Self-sufficiency
- A mixed market economy
- A labour-intensive economy
- Universal basic income vs universal basic services
- Monetary and fiscal co-ordination

We examine each of these in more detail and tie them in with the narrative of the preceding chapters so that a coherent story emerges. However, this is not the only story that I find compelling. There is another very recent one which may become a front runner, *Earth for All*.

Earth for All: A Survival Guide for Humanity, with multiple authors, emerges from the good work done by The Club of Rome, a group of concerned experts and philanthropists. They first came to fame, or perhaps infamy, with the publication of *The Limits to Growth*, way back in 1972.

The Limits to Growth, with Donella Meadows as the lead author, summarised the results of a group of systems researchers working out of the Massachusetts Institute of Technology (MIT) in the United States of America (USA). They were the first people to build dynamic computer simulations of how Earth's systems work. The scenarios they ran showed that with business-as-usual, we would hit the limits to economic growth on Earth and face collapse around about the middle of this century. It caused massive controversy and became a runaway bestseller.

Close on 50 years later, we are still on track for *The Limits to Growth* business-as-usual scenarios. To be able to predict a future scenario 50 years ahead is nothing short of remarkable. The book's computer simulations seem to fit well with reality. And this is one of the main reasons why I find their updated dynamic simulations of our current situation so compelling. The current team of Earth for All have by trial and error found the interventions which will be most effective in turning around our current situation:

- Ending poverty
- Addressing gross inequality
- Empowering women
- Making our food system healthy for people and ecosystems
- Transitioning to clean energy

While the headings are different to those of the BGND, the underlying assumptions, processes, and policies have much in common. A process of convergent evolution perhaps?

Unfortunately, I believe that, despite all their considerable strengths, both the BGND and Earth for All share a similar weakness. They lack concrete suggestions for how to achieve the political power needed to implement their proposals.

However, the central thrust of this book, the Citizens' Mandate for Change, is complementary to both proposals, because it provides a way of achieving the necessary political power. So, if you, like me, think the Mandate could work, BGND and Earth for All's lack of concrete suggestions is not a major stumbling block.

Whatever emerges from the Mandate in practice, it will probably provide a unifying pathway that combines the best elements of both a GND and Earth for All.

Chapter Eight
Transformation at National and Global Levels

If the Mandate does become an idea whose time has come, and of course you help to decide whether that is so, then it will spread globally. What might the main steps of this process be? One significant step will be when the first country achieves enough votes to change its political and economic systems to the new models.

I think this is most likely to be in a democracy with its own sovereign currency, that is, its own money supply. This important first step will boost the credibility of the new approach, and lower the threshold for other countries also to make the transition. It will begin a virtuous circle of growing international confidence in the new approach.

A second major step will be when a majority of the G20, the top twenty economic powers who control 80% of the global economy, come on board with the new systems. This threshold opens the space to take a fresh look at the present system of global governance. This hasn't happened since the Bretton Woods Conference at the end of the Second World War and is arguably long overdue.

We cover a brief overview of the present system of world governance, and explore some important ideas for designing a form of global governance that fits the needs of the current global situation. Included is the idea of a democratically elected United Citizens as an alternative option to the United Nations.

This leads on to looking at how the global financial systems would need to be changed to be fit for the purpose of resolving the major global issues. We will need to explore redesigning the global monetary supply, so that it supports the transformation of the global economy. This section includes the concept of a true international currency, as proposed by leading economist, John Maynard Keynes, to replace the dollar and to stabilise international trade.

The last part of the chapter maps out global wealth and income distribution and how to pay for the huge transformational changes we will need to make over something like a ten-year timescale.

Chapter Nine
Thinking in Systems for Systems That Work

Since we will have to look at major systems changes to escape the collapse that business-as-usual leads to, this chapter gives an overview of the systems-thinking skills which will be essential for the coming transformation.

It begins by introducing some of the building blocks of systems thinking, before moving onto the important work of Donella Meadows. She made the point that you can intervene in different places in any system, and these can be thought of as different levels of intervention. Other things being equal, interventions at different levels will have different degrees of leverage or effectiveness. We'll look at practical examples of interventions at some of the main levels.

I'll introduce nine of the most important ones, beginning with those that have the least leverage, to those that have the most. Leverage is simply the idea of how big the effect of an intervention, or change, is on the behaviour of the whole system.

Interventions at the lower levels are necessary and can be relatively fast to implement. However, intervening at the higher levels, such as changing the purpose of the system, are more effective, but will meet with more resistance. At the highest levels of effectiveness are the assumptions we often unconsciously bring to our thinking about the world. We'll look at some of the common assumptions of our culture which Donella Meadows considered to be both wrong and very dangerous.

The chapter also covers an overview of some of the main systems thinking approaches which are currently in use and their different strengths. When covering each of these disciplines I'll include books for those who want to dig deeper. The chapter ends by outlining the emerging new synthesis of applied systems thinking, a necessary skillset for the journey ahead of us.

Chapter Ten
The Human Predicament Revisited

Having explored the kinds of change that are both possible and necessary if we are to survive our present crises, we look back at the threats we mapped out in the first chapter. Here I'll assume that the Citizens' Mandate, or perhaps something else which can do the same job, does lift off and grows exponentially. How far would ten years of global transformation, along the lines which have been outlined here, take us in resolving each of the main threats?

We run through each of the threats in order, starting with the climate crisis and carbon dioxide levels. Fossil fuels will have been banned, or taxed so much that they will be little used, as we head for net zero emissions. Net zero emissions are when all greenhouse gases entering the atmosphere are balanced by those removed.

Three other main projects will have either taken place, or be well under way. The first is massive reforestation across the planet. The second is the transformation of agricultural practices to reabsorb carbon into the soil. And the third is the development of the other carbon drawdown technologies outlined in the book *Drawdown: The Most Comprehensive Plan Ever Proposed to Reverse Global Warming* edited by Paul Hawken.

The combined effect of these projects will be that the levels of carbon dioxide in the atmosphere will be broadly stabilised for the first time. Either the levels will still be above the stabilisation point, but decreasing, or they will have stabilised. In the best-case scenario, they will actually be decreasing and greenhouse gas emissions will be net negative. We need this to restore the climate to normal.

Similarly, as transformed global political and economic systems move us more into Kate Raworth's safe and sustainable space for humanity, the loss of biodiversity slows down, halts, and then biodiversity begins to increase again.

We will be looking at re-wilding up to half of the Earth's land surface. How? Mainly by reversing the damage that the current agribusiness systems are causing. One huge impact comes from a recent revolution in food production. We now have the ability to use sunlight and green electricity to brew nutritious high protein from naturally occurring soil bacteria in vats. And, yes, it tastes fine as a flour for cooking.

But the main point is this: as a way of producing protein, it uses only 1-2% of the land area that soya, our most protein intensive crop, uses. Currently, 70% of our farmland is used to produce animals for protein, or food-stock such as soya to feed those animals. With just this one innovation we can, in principle, free up two-thirds of the world's farmland for re-wilding. This is truly remarkable!

The rest of this chapter goes systematically though all of the main threats covered in the first chapter. And the good news is this: the kind of transformational changes we need to make in our complex global systems can resolve, or at least minimise, all the main threats that we face.

This is so because most of our problems are caused by the systems by which we run our human affairs. Once we change how the systems work, the problems begin to fall away. The new systems lead to improving wellbeing both for us humans and our planet. Nothing is guaranteed, but the path of greatest hope becomes much clearer.

Chapter Eleven
Back to You

All of the book up to this chapter has focussed mainly on the external world. And yet, that is only half the story. We each live in our inner world of ongoing subjective experience, our thoughts and feelings. But there is more to it than that. Just as the outer world brings into being experiences in our inner world, so our inner world brings into being experiences in our outer world in a dance of continual interaction. A brief explanation follows of epistemology, how we know what we know, and why it matters.

Most books of this kind studiously ignore the workings of our inner worlds. This chapter explores them. You could think of it as a guide to how to live well in a world gone mad. It draws on my experiences of teaching the inner skills of wellbeing over many decades, and I offer you the best of what emerged in mutual learning with my students.

Included are some guidelines on how to reduce the stresses caused by living in a world that is not always user-friendly. Also there are a set of skills, or processes, for developing your wellbeing. I call this a personal evolution process, for want of a better name. You may be familiar with some of these skills, but probably not all.

These skills or processes are simple to describe, generally work quite well, and are rewarding. But, like anything worthwhile, they can be challenging, at least initially. There are also some core principles for keeping your body, mind, emotions and spirit well-nourished.

My intention in this chapter is to balance the narrative of change we need in our external world with some of the skills for change in the inner world. The purpose is that you feel better equipped personally to look at, and engage with, the disturbing situations we all face. Also that you become clearer on what you are drawn to do as your personal part in helping to turn our problems around.

None of us can do everything, perish the thought, and nor do we need to. But all of us can do something and, if you and others are happy to include the Citizens' Mandate in your 'something', then that may be all that it takes.

Chapter Twelve
Conclusion: Your Part in Changing the World

Here, I pull together the threads of the narrative we have woven with a brief overview of the book to keep the main points as clear as possible. It's not always easy to see the wood for the trees.

After this, the main theme is to focus on action, and your potential part in this shared journey. I've included an exercise to help clarify what you are most drawn to do.

We revisit the Citizens' Mandate for Change for the last time. I've reviewed some of the main advantages that this approach has when done in addition to, or instead of, any of the more usual approaches. There is an initial outline of many of the different options and projects for action which may emerge as the Mandate lifts off and becomes a movement for change.

Movements for change are prone to many different kinds of 'elephant traps'. To minimise these risks, I've chosen as an exemplar one of the most effective movements for change in recent times. Rick Falkvinge founded the Pirate Party, which spread to 70 countries with a negligible budget. It was successful in getting new politicians elected to Parliament.

In his book, *Swarmwise: The Tactical Manual to Changing the World*, he outlines the principles of self-organisation. Based on his experience, he takes us through some of the most effective ways to develop a mass movement from scratch. He covers in practical detail much of what does, and doesn't, work. I summarise some of the main ideas that we can learn from.

My book is unusual in that it attempts to combine the best ideas from some of the world's leading thinkers and writers. Together, I believe they offer our most hopeful way forward. I've tried to make it all as engaging and as clear as possible. And I find what has emerged from their best thinking is both plausible, credible, and compelling.

I believe the Citizens' Mandate for Change is the single most powerful thing each of us can do because it really does have the potential to change everything. For together we *can* change the world.

However, this book is written for you, and what really interests me is whether *you* find it plausible, credible and even compelling. So, time to begin.

Chapter One
Are We Doomed?

The human predicament and the threats we face

I'd been researching a book on the climate crisis and all the other major problems we face, looking for the best way through them, the path of greatest hope. Was there a way though? What would it look like? Or are we doomed? At first it was very depressing. The more I learned, the more overwhelming it seemed to be. Later, I became more hopeful.

In this first chapter I'll look at the main threats we face, not just the climate crisis. Why? Because to deal with our fears we first have to look them in the face. However, all this makes seriously grim reading. So first, a repeat of the mental health warning from the Introduction.

If you are already deeply concerned about what the future holds, and it causes you anxiety, do not read this chapter first! Either start with Chapter Two, or perhaps Chapter Ten.

And again, if you are well versed in the 'doom literature', then jump straight to Chapter Two. From there on, this book is designed to be read in sequence as the narrative of hope is developed.

Civilisation collapse

There is no question that civilisations can and do collapse. Of the 300 main ones over the last 5,000 years, almost all have been and gone. They last around 300 years on average, then they collapse.

There's some interesting research which throws new light on the main reasons for collapse. This research was based on a cross-disciplinary model, called Handy, short for Human and Nature Dynamical. It showed two main features leading to collapse:

"the stretching of resources due to the strain placed on the ecological carrying capacity"

and

"the economic stratification of society into Elites (rich) and Masses (poor)"

The research concluded that these two main features have played a central role in the process of collapse of the vast majority of past civilisations. These two features fit well with two of our biggest problems. We have exceeded the planet's carrying capacity for carbon dioxide, and financial inequality is at an historical high. If we put the beginning of industrial civilisation around the 1830s in England, then we've pretty much had our 300-year run, unless we deal with our current problems.

The climate crisis

If you are not up to speed with the climate crisis, one of the best books has been created by Greta Thunberg. Called *The Climate Book*, it is a comprehensive overview by many separate authors who are all leading experts in their specialised fields. Another classic, and a relatively early one, is *This Changes Everything* by Naomi Klein.

Global average temperatures are currently more than 1.2°C above pre-industrial levels. 2023 has been the hottest year on record, at 1.48°C up, and the hottest year for 120,000 years. This spike in global temperatures was caused in part by El Niño warming the Pacific Ocean. An average of 1.5°C is expected to be reached within the next five years. The world record monthly average global temperature of 17.18°C was recorded on July 4th 2023. Just after this, our oceans hit a record high of 20.96°C.

July 2023 was our hottest month for more than some 120,000 years. Our best predictions currently put us on track for at least 2.7°C of global warming, even if all current agreements on reduction of greenhouse gasses were to be met.

In researching the climate crisis, perhaps the most depressing reading was *Our Final Warning, Six Degrees of Climate Emergency* by Mark Lynas. It is also a powerful wake-up call. He combines the best of climate modelling and geological research to map out what each degree of climate warming will mean to us in practice.

Six degrees of warming

Just how bad can it be? We are already at 1.2°C of global warming and know full well the extreme climate events this is subjecting us to. 2°C will place severe stress on most societies, cause markedly increased migration, and destroy a range of natural ecosystems from coral reefs to rainforests. Significant sea level rise begins.

At 3°C the stability of human civilisation is imperilled. By 4°C the full-scale collapse of human societies will probably have happened, accompanied by the worst biosphere mass extinctions of the last one hundred million years.

At 5°C, global temperatures are spiralling upwards relentlessly. The polar ice sheets are doomed, and sub-tropical rainforests will grow in Antarctica. Large areas of the planet are too hot for humans to live in. At wet bulb temperatures of 35°C, humans die.

With 6°C of warming we risk triggering a runaway greenhouse heating event that could herald the extinction of all life on Earth.

Some climate experts even believe our home planet may follow in the path of Venus with all water boiled off into space.

The climate tipping points

As if that weren't enough, there are all the tipping points at which the behaviour of our climate changes dramatically and permanently for the worse. A tipping point is simply the point at which the behaviour of a system makes a big, and often irreversible, change. There is significant uncertainty about tipping points, both in when they happen, and in just how bad the consequences are.

One of the best known is the melting of the Arctic sea ice. The poles are warming at about twice the rate of the rest of the planet. As the freshwater sea ice melts, the sea water that replaces it absorbs up to four times more heat, so the Arctic warms faster and the ice melts faster. A runaway vicious circle.

Another tipping point is the warming of the Arctic tundra. As the permafrost thaws, methane that has been stored underground is released. Methane has more than 80 times the warming effect of carbon dioxide, CO_2, over its first 20 years, although it is broken down faster than CO_2. As the atmosphere gets warmer, so more methane is released, creating another vicious circle.

And there are many other climate tipping points, some known, and almost certainly some unknown. Scary! What we do know is that as the global average temperature increases, we will hit more of these tipping points. The best estimate is that we will hit the tipping points for Arctic sea ice melting and tundra methane release somewhere between 1.5-2°C. This is a powerful motivation to stay below 1.5°C of warming.

Other main tipping points that we risk hitting by 2°C of warming include: Amazon rainforest dieback; permafrost melting; the collapse of the Greenland, West Antarctic, and two parts of the East Antarctic ice sheets; and the partial and/or total collapse of the Gulf Stream.

Research just published in the journal Nature shows that the Gulf Stream, called by scientists the Atlantic Meridional Overturning Circulation (AMOC), could hit a tipping point and switch off as early as 2025, although the average prediction is for 2050.

Here in the UK, the collapse of the Gulf Stream has been estimated to cause a fall in our average temperature of 3.6°C with the estimates ranging between 3°C and 8°C. This is comparable to Alaska. The effects of this would be dire and I don't like to think about it.

According to Our World in Data, ourworldindata.org, carbon dioxide causes about 74.4% of global warming. The balance is made up of methane (17.3%), nitrous oxide (6.2%) and small amounts of other gases (2.1%). Together they are known as the greenhouse gases.

You can track the amount of carbon dioxide in the atmosphere at https://www.co2.Earth/daily-co2. There are around 420 parts per million of CO_2 in the atmosphere now, compared to the background level of 280ppm before the industrial revolution. Somewhat worryingly, and despite all our efforts to date, the levels of CO_2 have continued to increase at much the same rate as the global economy continues to grow.

The nine environmental planetary boundaries

The climate crisis may be the best known of the environmental problems we have, but sadly it is just one among many others. This comprehensive assessment of all environmental risks comes from the pioneering work done by Johan Rockstrom and colleagues at the Stockholm Resilience Centre at Stockholm University since 2009.

They identified the nine main areas of environmental risk, and the safe zones that we must stay within to avoid catastrophes. The diagram on page 28 is the most recent update (2022). Below are the areas, starting with the highest risk, and moving through to the lowest.

The planetary boundaries

1. Novel entities
2. Biosphere integrity
3. Biogeochemical flows
4. Land-system change
5. Climate change
6. Freshwater change
7. Ocean acidification
8. Atmospheric aerosol loading
9. Stratospheric ozone depletion

What is most immediately striking about this list is that climate change is not number one. Why? Basically, this research looks at the risks of Earth's systems changing through crossing critical thresholds rather than directly at the risks to people. The media news, on the other hand, reports on visible phenomena which affect people directly. The effects of climate change are visible and obvious, while the effects on the other boundaries are less visible.

Planetary Boundaries

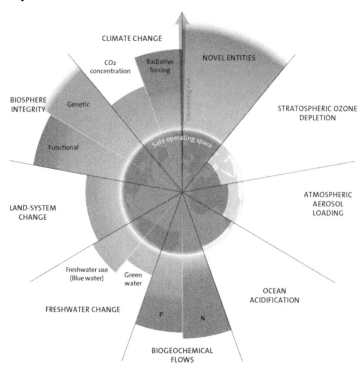

(Credit: "Azote for Stockholm Resilience Centre,
based on analysis in Richardson et al 2023")

It's worth noting that these nine boundaries are described separately,
but with the way that Earth's biophysical systems work, in practice
each one affects all the others, so that they are continually influencing
each other.

Novel entities

Plastics pollution has been in the news recently. However, novel
entities includes more than just plastics. There are some 350,000
chemical pollutants released into the environment at the rate of 10
million tons annually. Amongst these are plastics, pesticides, industrial

chemicals, antibiotics, and so on. Taken together, they have a devastating effect on the ecosystems of the world. As with aerosols, carbon dioxide, nitrogen and phosphorus, novel entities are increasing in proportion to economic growth. We are way outside their safe zone.

Biosphere integrity

This concerns our natural world. The integrity of our biosphere covers the loss of biodiversity and species extinctions. These are caused mainly by pollution, our increasing use of land for food, and our growing demand for water.

Biosphere integrity, like novel entities, is one of the areas of highest risk because our human civilisation is entirely dependent on the living world. The loss of parts of the natural world damages us both directly and indirectly. The collapse of the natural world would mean the end of civilisation as we know it. This may depend on unknown ecological tipping points. We are already well outside the safe zone in this area.

Biogeochemical flows

Biogeochemical flows are about the misuse of fertilisers by modern agribusiness. The flows of nitrogen and phosphorus into our river systems and the ocean are the third highest area of risk for our planet. Both these elements are produced and used on a massive scale as fertilisers for growing food.

Most of it is wasted as runoff into rivers and the oceans, where it causes high levels of pollution worldwide. Nitrogen and phosphorus pollution kill off aquatic species on an epic scale, causing algal blooms in rivers and massive dead zones in our oceans. Again, we are outside the safe zone.

Land-system change

More and more of our forests, grasslands and wetlands are being taken over for agricultural use. As the land used for agriculture continues to expand, this reduces biodiversity, releases more carbon as carbon dioxide into the atmosphere, and releases more nitrogen and phosphorus into our waterways and so into the sea. In this planetary boundary we are again outside the safe zone and well into the area of increasing risk.

Climate change

We have explored this previously, and it might have come as a surprise to you that this is not considered the highest area of risk by the Stockholm Resilience Centre who rank it fifth, but it is still well outside the safe operating space. For the following boundaries, we are in more of a grey area, because safe zone boundaries are merely an estimate.

Freshwater use

The availability of fresh water is closely linked to changes in the climate, yet the biggest pressure comes from our increasing use of water. Threats include the lowering of underground water tables by pumping water up for irrigation of crops, melting of the glaciers that feed so many of our main rivers, and nitrogen and phosphorus pollution. In addition, wars over water supply are a growing risk.

Half the world's population live in areas of water scarcity for at least one month per year, and we have recently exceeded the safe zone for this risk.

Ocean acidification

This is still just within the safe zone. However, around 40% of the carbon dioxide released is absorbed by the ocean. It dissolves in water, forming carbonic acid and making the seas more acidic; this situation is worsening fast.

Up to half our coral reefs, our oceanic canary-in-the-mine, are already gone. Many shellfish, plankton, and other species are under threat, and because of this we face a resulting collapse in fish stocks; fish is one of our main protein sources in food.

Atmospheric aerosol loading

You'll probably have heard of this one because it has been cropping up in the news. Aerosols are particles or droplets in the air, often called particulate matter.

Although still considered to be within the safe zone, the number of aerosols increases as the economy grows. They are thought to cause seven million premature deaths annually worldwide. Aerosols play a complex role in cloud formation and offset the heating effects of the various greenhouse gases.

Stratospheric ozone depletion

Ozone in the upper atmosphere protects us from the high levels of ultraviolet (UV) radiation from the sun. High levels of UV cause skin cancers in humans and damage to all forms of life exposed to them. The appearance of the Antarctic ozone hole alerted us to this problem and the Montreal Protocol in 1987 enabled us to keep ozone levels within the safe zone, an encouraging success story.

By the way, you've now made it halfway through this list of threats and you're still here. Well done! Let's go straight on to look at the other risks which we face.

What other main risks do we face?

The climate crisis and the other eight planetary boundaries cover the main risks that our growing economy poses for our planetary ecosystems.

However, since in this chapter we are looking all our fears in the face, it is worth having a quick look at the other risks we face. These can be grouped into three categories: natural, man-made, and other risks.

Natural risks

This simply means the risks that happen through natural, rather than man-made causes.

Asteroid or comet collisions

The potential catastrophe that gets the most press coverage is that of a collision with an asteroid or comet. Asteroids are lumps of metal or rock, whilst comets are rock surrounded by ice.

The best-known example is the asteroid that hit the Earth at the end of the Cretaceous period. This caused the mass extinction event which killed off the dinosaurs and all other animals over 5kg. It was 10 kilometres in diameter and threw enough dust into the atmosphere to cause a prolonged 'nuclear winter' effect by significantly dimming the sun.

Even an asteroid of 1 kilometre diameter threatens a global catastrophe. The National Aeronautics and Space Administration (NASA) in the USA has been tracking these asteroids for over twenty years. Fortunately, the chance of an asteroid of this size hitting the Earth in the next century is less than 1 in 120,000.

The probability of a strike by an asteroid of 10 kilometres or more is less than one in 250 million. In the greater scheme of things, this is perhaps not one of our biggest worries.

Supervolcano eruptions

Of more concern is a threat from under the Earth rather than above it, a supervolcano eruption. These do about the same amount of damage as a 1 kilometre asteroid strike. One of the best known supervolcano eruptions took place at Yellowstone in the USA over 600,000 years ago. Supervolcano events happen around once every 80,000 years.

So, this looks like a 1 in 80,000 annual risk, or 1 in 800 per century, but with a high degree of uncertainty. This is much more of a worry than asteroid strikes, but far less than that of a climate catastrophe.

By comparison, on the business-as-usual model, climate catastrophe and the collapse of global civilisation look highly likely within a few decades.

Stellar explosions

Some stars at the end of their lives explode and become supernovae, releasing an intense burst of energy. If near enough to the Earth, the gamma and cosmic radiation they release would damage the atmosphere. They would do this by producing nitrous oxides and dramatically eroding the ozone layer. This removal of ozone in turn would lead to a massive increase of UV radiation, with damage to all species. Fortunately, the chance of this is only about 1 in 2.5-5 million. So, this is another one that is not a significant worry.

If you want to know more, all the above figures are taken from Toby Ord's outstanding book, *The Precipice – Existential Risks and the Future of Humanity*. He also does a series of estimates of the risk from all natural causes combined, based on our past. His best guess is less than 0.05% per century, or a probability of under 1 in 2000 per century. However, he considers that these are dwarfed by human created risks which are 1,000 times larger. Let's take a look at these.

Anthropogenic risks

This simply means risks that are created by us, as distinct from the naturally occurring risks above.

Global thermonuclear war

It is often said that we have enough nuclear weapons to destroy the world many times over. This is simply not true, but the situation is complex. What would the effects be? It is true that billions would die, perhaps a majority of the population. The first effects are the deaths by nuclear flash, blast, and fires. Then come deaths by radiation poisoning. But the biggest killer would be the ensuing nuclear winter as the skies darken with dust, leading to mass starvation.

The global temperature would drop by an estimated 7°C for five years, then would gradually increase again over the next ten years. Most food plants would have too short a growing season to mature and the ensuing famine would kill most of the human population. But not all. So, the only good news here is that this is unlikely to be an extinction event for humanity.

The probability of global thermonuclear war is well-nigh impossible to estimate, but geopolitical tensions between nuclear powers directly and massively increase it. Even without this factor, there have been too many close calls for any degree of comfort.

The Doomsday Clock was created by the Bulletin of Atomic Scientists in 1947 to assess the risk of nuclear catastrophe. In 2023 it stands at 90 seconds to midnight. This is the highest level of risk it has ever shown.

An increase in the number of autocratic states and populist authoritarian leaders increases the risk of such an event, whereas the growth of democratic states decreases the risk.

Climate crisis

Although we've already looked at this one, I decided it was worth looking again. The dangers of the climate crisis are unique. The immediate threats are clear, and they steadily get more severe every year unless we find a way of resolving them. As Antonio Guterres, Secretary General of the UN said, he believes we are doomed with business-as-usual. His exact words from November 2022:

"At the present level [of emissions], we will be doomed. We are approaching tipping points, and tipping points that will make [climate change] irreversible. The damage that would not allow us to recover (sic)."

The saving grace here is that the effects of climate change happen in relatively slow motion. We still have time to turn things around if we act very soon, and on a massive collective scale. If we don't, the downside is the highly probable collapse of global civilisation. This is the strong argument for climate change being the biggest risk we currently face.

Overpopulation

Overall, global population is stabilising although, other things being equal, we are set to add another billion, or maybe two billion, to our present 7 billion. The main risk here is not so much the population itself, as the increasing consumption of fossil fuel energy and materials per head of population. This increasing consumption is what is directly feeding into exceeding our planetary boundaries.

Other future risks

You could argue that these other risks are also man-made, but I've decided to stick with Toby Ord's classification.

Pandemics

There is a strong case for including pandemics as human caused problems. The evidence is growing that our activities are increasing the risk of new and dangerous pandemics. The Covid pandemic has illustrated the profound effects these can have on society. In the case of Covid, the spread rate was high, but mercifully, the death rate was relatively low at around 1% of those infected.

One way we are increasing the risk of disease is our overuse of antibiotics; this actively selects for antibiotic resistant forms of diseases. Another is the killing and eating of wild animals infected with new diseases. A third is creating the conditions for new mutations of viruses which have both a high spread rate and mortality rate.

The Spanish Flu of 1918 killed around 100 million people; this was more than the number of those killed in the First World War. Probably the worst pandemic we know of was the Black Death of the fourteenth century caused by a bacterium, Yersina pestis. It is believed to have killed between a quarter and a half of all those infected in Europe alone.

Last, but not least, gene editing technologies such as CRISPR give us the capability of producing pandemics to order. One research lab controversially produced a variant of the H5N1 virus, related to bird flu, with a mortality rate of 60% in humans. This wasn't released and fortunately, even if it had escaped by accidental release, it had a low transmission rate.

The main risks of man-made pandemics come from the accidental release of a dangerous disease from a research lab, or their development and intentional use as bioweapons. Another risk is that they may be developed and used by terrorist groups. Overall, we are at high risk of serious future pandemics. This is one of the big ones.

Artificial intelligence

From its origins in 1956, the field of artificial intelligence has evolved rapidly. Like any technology, it can be a force for good or ill. Because of the vast potential of AI, this applies with a vengeance.

Looking at the downsides, in the short term perhaps the main one is displacing us humans from the workforce and causing widespread unemployment. Our present systems are not designed to cope with this. The problem arises from the development and use of current technologies which use deep neural network learning from massive datasets. These are based loosely on how the networks of nerves in the brain process information. ChatGPT was the first one to hit the news.

The field of artificial general intelligence (AGI) is being developed. It is possible, but not certain, that AGI may come to be in many respects more intelligent than humans. Experts in the field expect this to happen within a timeframe of a decade to a century. What are the risks then?

Most discussed is the risk of an AGI taking over control with its own agenda and eliminating us. Is this feasible? Well, it's certainly plausible. An AGI could take control of the internet and manipulate the images and words we see and hear. But how exactly would that control us?

If you think about it, some of the most damaging individuals in history, say Hitler, Stalin, or Genghis Khan, built their huge power base by using mainly words and images. This gave them physical power. So, this becomes a credible route by which an AGI could achieve world dominance. Not a pretty thought!

What is the risk of this happening? It is hard to know, but perhaps the main determining factor is the nature of the human culture in which AGI is developed. An authoritarian regime may actively develop an AGI to amplify its own power. Such a regime could unwittingly release it in the world not realising the AGI had the power to take down the authoritarian regime, and itself become the dominating world power.

Perhaps the main risk of AI and AGI comes from unknown future applications. This brings us to the next threat, that of authoritarian dictatorships.

Dystopian scenarios

A dystopia is the opposite of utopia; it is a society of great suffering or injustice. Take Hitler's Germany as an example. If he had won World War II, and then gone on to achieve world dominance, we might have seen a world locked into an authoritarian and totalitarian order of the kind outlined by George Orwell in his classic book *1984*. This is one of the main potential risks posed by dystopian scenarios.

A much more plausible scenario runs at the level of the nation state. Under our present system, trust in governments and democracy continues to decline to record lows. This improves the prospects for populist and ultra-nationalistic authoritarian leaders. With the help of financing by vested interests and corrupt social media disinformation campaigns, these leaders can, and do, achieve power. Look no further than all the populist authoritarian leaders in nominal democracies at the moment.

Their standard playbook is to blame powerless scapegoats such as immigrants or other minorities, to distort or defraud elections in their own favour, and to attempt to lock themselves into power permanently. At the same time they borrow internationally, and defraud the state of huge amounts of money which they transfer to tax havens.

Think of many of the leaders and ex-leaders of Africa states and the Global South who, after being in power, leave their countries to pay off their lethal debts indefinitely. I say lethal, because the endemic poverty they create kills millions through famine and disease.

Apart from unnecessary suffering and injustice, there is perhaps a bigger risk. The way the authoritarian mind works tends towards over-simplistic black and white thinking, and away from the complexities of the real world. It is much easier for the authoritarian mind to deny and ignore the climate crisis than to acknowledge it and have to take the steps to deal with it. Again, think of the populist and authoritarian leaders who have increased the environmental damage in so many places around the world including the Amazonian rainforests.

In my view dystopian scenarios are one of the most serious risks that we face. This is because populist leaders tend to have authoritarian minds, serve their own short-term interests, and are usually deniers of the threats we face.

Other risks

We are not quite done. There are other risks too. Nanotechnology, or technology working at the molecular level, is one. As we develop new machines working at this level, new possibilities for good and ill arise.

Or consider non-terrestrial life forms. In popular imagination this takes the form of alien invasion, H. G. Wells's *The War of the Worlds*, and so on. It is entirely credible that there are intelligent life forms out there, and it is possible that some of them may have bad intentions for us. This might, of course, be no more than paranoia on our part...

With SETI, the Search for Extra-Terrestrial Intelligence, we may find them, and this could turn out badly. But perhaps more likely is the chance of discovering alien micro-organisms in our exploration of the planets and accidentally bringing them back to Earth with unintended bad consequences.

There is action we can take

For nearly all of these risks, there is action we can take to mitigate them. We'll explore some of these actions in the rest of this book. The only real exceptions are supervolcanoes and stellar explosions.

However, to take effective action against the risks we face, we would need benign and effective governance systems for our planet. Sadly, we are nowhere near having such a governance system yet. How could we move in this direction? The next part of this book looks at the causes of our problems and then the most promising pathways for us to take.

And by the way, congratulations for hanging in there as we looked at the potential downsides! Most of this doesn't have to happen. We'll get increasingly more hopeful from here on in.

Chapter Two
What Are the Fundamental Causes?

Before you read this chapter, I'd like you to pause briefly. If I were to ask you what you think are the basic causes of our problems, what would you say? Having thought briefly, you might want to compare and contrast your thoughts with mine as you read on.

Human nature or human systems?

Many people think we have created these problems because we are basically too short-sighted and greedy. This belief reflects the notion that human nature is the fundamental cause. I don't buy this.

There is much work from the fields of anthropology, archaeology, psychology, and the social sciences which supports the notion that our capacities for altruism and cooperation exceed our capacities for being short-sighted and self-centred. One of the most compelling cases for this was made by David Graeber and David Wengrow in their impressive and enjoyable book, *The Dawn of Everything – A New History of Humanity*.

My friend and colleague, Sarah Smith, asks this question: "Why do we collectively and consistently keep producing results that nobody wants?" She points out that none of us wake up in the morning and think: "How can I make the climate crisis worse today?" or "How can I make inequality worse?" So how come we are so good at creating unwanted results?

We seem to be enmeshed in a mess of complex systems that consistently produce these unwanted results, these unintended consequences. If we want different results, then we need to change these systems. I find this approach more compelling than the notion that human nature is the problem. And it is arguably easier to change our systems than to change human nature. Let's take a closer look at the systems which have created the problems we face.

Why are we creating these problems for ourselves?

What exactly are these systems which are producing unintended consequences of such magnitude that they threaten both the collapse of our ecosystems and of human civilisation itself? These unintended consequences are the stuff of which much of Chapter One is made. Here, we'll be pondering how and why we are creating these problems for ourselves.

Our economic systems

Centre stage must be our economic systems. The goal of any economic system is often loosely stated as promoting the economic wellbeing of a nation's citizens. The main actors in an economic system are the business organisations in which most of us work.

They have served us well in the past in many ways, and have brought the majority of the population more wealth and wellbeing than our ancestors would have believed possible. However, our businesses have worked within the system we call capitalism. Along with the development of different forms of capitalism over the last five centuries, there have also been significant downsides. Think here of slavery, colonialism, or environmental exploitation. Why does our economic system create our problems?

Fundamental flaws

There are major flaws in our basic capitalist economic model. I will mention just four here. The first is economic growth. As the economist, Kenneth Boulding remarked:

"Anyone who believes exponential growth can go on forever in a finite world is either a madman or an economist."

The second flaw is what economists refer to as 'externalities', that is all those things that are not accounted for in the economic systems of our economy. Carbon dioxide emissions are but one example of an externality. Another economist, Sir Nicholas Stern, famously said in his review to the Royal Economic Society:

"Climate change is the result of the greatest market failure that the world has seen."

For the third flaw, I quote Robert Kennedy in his famous speech about Gross National Product (GNP):

"Yet the gross national product does not allow for the health of our children, the quality of their education or the joy of their play. It does not include the beauty of our poetry or the strength of our marriages, the intelligence of our public debate or the integrity of our public officials. It measures neither our wit nor our courage, neither our wisdom nor our learning, neither our compassion nor our devotion to our country, it measures everything in short, except that which makes life worthwhile."

And for the fourth, I will include this flaw. Economics discounts the future. Beyond the relatively near future, nothing has any value. This reflects what psychologists call 'present bias'. Our economic system is extremely near-sighted. It will always sacrifice a future benefit for a present gain. In the context of the climate crisis, need I say more?

I could go on in this vein, but I will spare you the other dysfunctionalities of the so-called 'dismal science'. Enough to say there are catastrophic design flaws built into our present economic systems and this is why they create our problems.

Our political systems

This brings us to another 'why' question. Why are our economic systems so flawed? The short answer is because the rules of the economic system are made by the political system. If politicians changed the rules of the economic system, then the economic system would change how it works. Why, then, has the political system created an economic system that is so terminally dysfunctional?

So far, I have done my best to keep things as simple as possible. This is known as the parsimony principle. It is basic to all science and tells us to choose the simplest explanation that fits the evidence.

But now, things begin to get more complicated. In addressing the question of why the political system has created an economic system that is not fit for purpose, there is no single cause, there are a number of different contributory causes. Here I will cover some of the main ones, so let's consider these.

Causes of political dysfunction

First, most politicians do not have an in-depth understanding of how economic systems actually work. The minority who do have some background, such as a degree in 'Philosophy, Politics and Economics', will have mainly studied orthodox economics of the neoliberal tradition. This is exceedingly narrow compared to the many other different schools of heterodox economics. These include evolutionary economics, ecological economics and complexity economics. They all have different assumptions, often widely so.

Additionally, I could find no evidence of any politician having a significant background in applied systems thinking. Since our economic system is a system, this means politicians tend to be blind to the systemic effects of their policies. This is commonplace and in my view it is a serious limitation.

Also, politicians, like all groups of people, are subject to a phenomenon known as 'groupthink'. Groupthink is when members of small cohesive groups tend to unconsciously accept a viewpoint or conclusion that represents a perceived group consensus. They do this whether or not each individual believes the consensus to be valid, correct, or optimal.

For example, many politicians think that economic growth is the best way to solve all our problems, and that neoliberal economics is the best way to achieve such growth. However, neoliberal economics is perhaps the most extreme version of capitalism. It is more the cause of our different problems than the solution to them. Most politicians also think that compared to growth, climate change is a less important problem.

Rebecca Willis, who has researched this phenomenon with many politicians here in the UK, gives a detailed account of how this happens in practice in her unique book *Too Hot to Handle – The Democratic Challenge of Climate Change*. She explains why our politicians' response to climate change is so weak. There are many different factors at play, but a major one is the so called 'Overton Window'.

The Overton Window
Political groupthink goes a long way to explaining an important phenomenon in politics known as the 'Overton Window'. The Overton Window is named after the American policy analyst, Joseph Overton, who originated the idea. It frames the range of policies that politicians consider to be politically feasible, the range of political discourse, and how policies change over time. Any new idea in politics

moves though a predictable sequence: from unthinkable, to radical, to acceptable, to popular, and only finally to policy.

Take the climate crisis as an example. On the Overton Window spectrum, where would you say politicians put actually solving the climate crisis, rather than just talking about it? The direction of travel is clear, but political groupthink and the Overton Window partly explain why progress has been so slow.

Denial

Third, almost all of us are in significant denial about the scale and significance of the most serious problems we face. It is a common coping strategy. You could argue that denial is not a direct cause, but it is certainly a big part of the problem, the elephant in the room even.

A recent (2023) survey of seven main European countries, including Britain, showed that nearly 20% of their population believe climate change is not caused by humans, and nearly 5% believe climate change is not happening. For the massive majority, climate change is real, human caused, and probably the biggest threat we face. We need to take appropriate action on it as a top priority. But we deny it when we don't talk about it because it's too uncomfortable. The media deny it when they too don't talk about it and distract us with trivia instead. For politicians, perhaps the denial lies more in not taking action at anything like the scale clearly required.

The main cause?

There is a fourth, and perhaps main cause, of why the political system has created and maintains an economic system that is not fit for purpose: vested interests. Big organisations with vested interests, such as big oil, constantly invest in lobbying politicians to look after their interests. The sums invested in lobbying are huge.

The lobbying industry is worth £1.9 billion in the UK, with MPs approached by lobbyists as many as 100 times per week. I was struck by one estimate I read which put the return on these lobbying investments as often being around 200:1! On top of this there is an open revolving door of powerful and rich people moving between high levels of the business world and the political world. A revolving groupthink door?

If you take lobbying, vested interests, the revolving door, groupthink, denial, and the Overton Window all working together, they are quite sufficient to explain why governments promote economic systems which are so flawed, and fail us on the climate crisis. Whilst our economic systems are dysfunctional for most citizens and dysfunctional for the global ecosystems, they are very functional for the rich and powerful elite, who grow ever richer and more powerful.

This dynamic 'locks in' the existing system and explains why it is so exceedingly difficult to change it, even when it is going to cause the collapse of civilisation. We are locked into a system that is extremely good at maintaining its own structure. In systems-thinking terms, this is known as an ultrastable system.

That doesn't, of course, mean that it can't be changed. Rebecca Willis highlights the need to ramp up our levels of democratic engagement at every level to address this core issue. But more of this in the following chapter. Here we have looked at the different levels of causation of our major problems, with particular regard to the climate crisis. However we are still looking for the underlying causes.

Why are our political systems so flawed?

We have looked at how our political system is not fundamentally fit for purpose, but not why it is so. In this quest for the root cause of our many problems, I want to again explore why. Once more, complexity rules, and there are many causes. But here are a few of the main ones to ponder.

One of them is historical causation. Representative democracy grew, like Topsy, without design or planning. Or to put it more accurately, it developed largely by historical accident. And it developed as the bedfellow of the earlier versions of capitalism in which the rich and the powerful ruled. Back in the times when representative democracies came into being, both in the UK and the USA, the common wisdom was that the mass of people were unfit to vote, let alone rule. Note that presupposition well. Representative democracy was designed to work to keep power and wealth in the hands of the few. It still does this, and it does it very effectively.

I think another causative factor is simply having political parties. If we didn't have political parties, we would be spared such a strong ideological factor in determining policies. This has a direct bearing on the current predominance of neoliberal economics, which is basically just an ideology. To be clear, an ideology is a system of ideas and ideals, especially one which forms the basis of economic or political theory and policy.

An additional cause is the way in which political parties are funded. On the right wing, this is predominantly by the rich and powerful. This further distorts the political system and is the equivalent of the lobbying we looked at earlier.

A further cause is that most of the press are right-wing, and are owned by billionaires who clearly have vested interests. They promote the parties that support the neoliberal ideology which in turn supports their interests. The predominantly right-wing press gives no voice to any significant alternatives, or if it mentions them, it is only to ridicule them.

Democracy, the worst form of government, except...

Some argue that a lack of the ability to imagine a better political system is a fundamental cause. The quote often attributed to Winston Churchill 'Democracy is the worst form of government, except for all the others.' embodies this notion. As a matter of interest, what he actually said was:

"Many forms of Government have been tried, and will be tried in this world of sin and woe. No one pretends that democracy is perfect or all-wise. Indeed, it has been said that democracy is the worst form of Government except for all those other forms that have been tried from time to time...."

I believe we can design and create more effective forms of democracy. Many of them already exist elsewhere, and we'll explore these soon. Being able to imagine a better form of democracy for a better future is necessary, but we will still need a practical way of bringing it about.

The last cause I want to mention here, to round off this section on underlying causes, is this. Unlike the others above, this one is a cause that is primarily internal to us as individuals. The following may seem obvious, but I believe it has profound implications.

We act as we do because we think as we do, and our thinking is often driven by our unconscious assumptions. I will come back to this idea of some of our 'out of conscious' belief systems being key drivers when we explore the different kinds of positive futures that we are able to create.

Why do we produce results nobody wants?

Returning to my friend Sarah Smith's question, "Why do we collectively and consistently keep producing results that nobody wants?", the answer is looking like this. Our economic system is the main cause of the unintended social and environmental problems, which continue to get worse in direct proportion to the growth of the economy. And our political system is the fundamental cause of creating and maintaining this flawed economic system.

In summary, the political system is unfit for purpose for a number of reasons: it evolved to serve the interests of the powerful and wealthy, it is based on political parties mainly funded by elites, it is supported by the right-wing press, it hasn't yet been replaced by a better system, and our unconscious assumptions often play a part in maintaining it.

Whether you agree with this thinking on the fundamental cause of our problems, I believe how we each see the causes is important because it will tend to determine where we look for solutions. In the next chapter I want to explore with you this central issue: what on Earth can we do about the mess we're in?

Chapter Three
What Can We Do? The Citizens' Mandate

You might want to take a moment and ask yourself this non-trivial question. If you had the power to do anything, what would you do to bring about meaningful change? A tricky one indeed!

We've looked at the problems, we've looked at the causes, and now it's time to start looking for potential solutions, or perhaps resolutions. For the sake of simplicity, I'll start by focussing on just one problem, and probably our biggest one, the climate crisis. We will get to the others in due course.

What can you do?

So what can you do, individually, and collectively with others? On the individual level, you can do whatever is within your power to reduce your carbon footprint. You've heard it all before: recycle, install LEDs, turn the heating down, insulate, eat more meat alternatives, car pool or drive an electric car, stop flying for holidays, and so on. In the workplace you can argue for more carbon friendly policies, services, and products. All this is all good and necessary, but sadly, not sufficient.

Collectively, you can join the many different movements for change, and there are literally millions of them, like Extinction Rebellion, Fridays for Future, Just Stop Oil, Greenpeace, and so many others. This too is good and necessary, but not yet sufficient.

You can become more democratically engaged. Join political parties you are aligned with, or movements for political change such as proportional representation with the Electoral Reform Society. Perhaps one of the most effective things you can do is write to your MP or go to one of their surgeries. They probably pay more attention to individual communication than to mass petitions. Yet again, this is good and may be necessary, but it is still not sufficient.

So what else can you do?

The question becomes, what would be sufficient? When dealing with change in complex systems, the most effective strategy is to build a rich picture of the system you are looking at, then to focus on the places where a small difference could make a really big change in the behaviour of the whole system.

This is called looking for leverage, the difference that makes the difference. When you find the point of leverage that looks most promising, then you clarify what exactly you can do that could trigger change in the system. You try it and see if it works. If it doesn't, you adjust it, recycle, and try again.

Applying this to our situation, it seems to me that the political system is the one to go for. Worldwide surveys have repeatedly shown that anywhere between 60% and 90% of the population is dissatisfied with our current political systems, whilst only 6% is happy with the status quo. There is low and falling confidence in governments. Rates of anxiety and depression are at record high levels and are growing; the majority feel hopeless and powerless to change things.

When I talk with the people I know, most now believe we are doomed. However, there is a flipside to this. Looking at the positive side, the worse things get, the greater the social motivation for meaningful change. It may well be that it takes major crises to provoke major transformations. This provides potentially fertile territory.

Another thought here. One of the downsides of believing we are doomed is that you need take no action about it, because there is no point. There is precisely the same downside to believing that all will be well, or, for that matter, denying that climate change is a problem; you need take no action.

However, without collective action, we *are* doomed! So it seems that we need to believe the dangers are real, but also that there is a way through and that there is something we can do. What might that be?

Political will and memes

In reading the literature, one of the most common themes or tropes is that we lack the 'political will' to make the changes we need to transcend our challenges. I wondered, what exactly is political will? And how could we manifest it in a more tangible form? I remembered my mentor in systems thinking, Stafford Beer, lamenting that people have no collective voice. How could we have a collective political voice? This thought has stayed with me over the decades.

Another thread going around in my mind was meme theory, or memetics. In the common culture, memes have come to mean things like video clips going viral. The roots of meme theory are rather different. The term was introduced by Richard Dawkins back in 1976 in his well-known book, *The Selfish Gene*.

He thought of memes as being the cultural parallel of biological genes and saw them as replicating themselves in human cultures. A meme in his original sense is any pattern of internal thought and external behaviour that is capable of spreading by person-to-person transmission in human societies. When you think about it this includes pretty much any behaviour which is capable of spreading.

Susan Blackmore took this idea and developed it further than anyone else in her book, *The Meme Machine*. She makes a strong case for meme theory having greater explanatory power for human behaviour than genetics. Her hypothesis is that the human brain evolved as a vehicle, a 'meme machine', for the transmission of the fittest patterns of thought and behaviour in human cultures. By this spreading of the fittest ideas, human cultures evolved. This seems to me to make sense.

New political memes of transformation?

I wondered if it might be theoretically possible to design a new meme, or set of memes, that had the capacity to change our political systems. I couldn't let go of this idea. What might these memes of political transformation look like? Although I've worked in change professionally for some 40 or so years, one day I found myself suddenly noticing the obvious. In all matters of change, there are always three central questions: From what? To what? And how specifically?

Could the questions of change become memes for political transformation? What might they look like? How would they work? How would they replicate? As I continued to dwell on these questions, I eventually had one of those 'aha' moments when it all came together. Bear with me here.

A majority of people are feeling profoundly dissatisfied, powerless and hopeless about the current political system. Hope comes from wanting something and having a way of getting there. A collective voice could provide the power to get there. Writing to your MP gives you a little influence, but a lot of people writing to their MPs could provide a more powerful voice. However, if we all just wrote whatever we thought, it would be rather mixed and muddled and any core messages would get lost in all the noise.

The origins of the Citizens' Mandate for Change

But, if what we wrote was aligned around the three core questions of change, the central messages could be made abundantly clear. However, only MPs would know what those central messages were, and then only if they took the time and trouble to figure out what a lot of people were saying in common. This is a non-trivial task. Furthermore, we wouldn't know what our collective central messages were.

But suppose we all sent copies of what we were saying to our MPs to a website and it stored them up? Then, if we could summarise our separate answers to the three core questions of change, we would have both a collective political voice to speak to politicians with, and we and they would know what our central messages were. If this idea spread widely, it could then become a viral meme with the potential to change the culture and the political system.

This seemed really promising, so I did some research to see if this idea already existed. I couldn't find it, which surprised me, so it looked like this was new thinking. It was both innovative and an intervention which could be tested in practice.

What exactly would the three questions need to be? The first question has to specify 'From what?' and focus on the main issues that need dealing with. The answer is going to be sent to your MP and to the Citizen's Mandate website, **citizensmandate.com**, so the most concise way of asking it seemed to be this question:

What are the main issues you are concerned about?

The second question, 'To what?', is about our preferred future. So I aimed this at the kind of society that we ideally want to be living in:

What kind of society would you prefer to be living in?

The last question, 'How specifically?' is focussed on the specific action steps, the changes that politicians could make, to address our main concerns and move us closer to our ideal society. This question became:

What changes do you want our government to make?

I tested these questions out with friends by asking them if they would be happy to give their written answers. 24 out of 25 were. The 25th was a natural contrarian and refused to give any reason for refusing… You win some, you lose some!

The next problem was how to meaningfully combine the answers in a way that was intuitively obvious. This was in the days before ChatGPT, the AI that could quickly do a written summary of any desired length. The answer seemed to be 'word clouds'. Originally called Wordle, this is software that will read any text you give it. It then finds the most common words and phrases, and prints them as an image, a cloud of words, with the most common appearing in the middle as the biggest ones, and the rest surrounding them in decreasing size. The advantage of this is that you can see the main messages at a glance.

I tested this and it worked fine. Interestingly the two biggest phrases it showed in my small sample were 'climate change' and 'financial inequality'. Alongside of ChatGPT type summaries, which could be expanded to whatever length worked best, we could summarise what we were saying collectively in two quite different ways.

Next, I was curious to know whether the idea could spread, so I asked my friends to talk to their friends and let me know how it went. The results were encouraging; their friends almost always responded positively and wanted to know more about it. I still remember one friend pinning me down and wanting to know very precisely what the Citizens' Mandate was. There are five key components.

The five elements of the Citizens' Mandate for Change

The Citizens' Mandate for Change has these five main elements:

One

It is a political mandate of your wishes empowering your Member of Parliament to act on your behalf. The idea of a mandate is similar to making your wishes clear in your Will.

Two

Your Mandate is made up of your answers, of around 100 words each, to three key questions:

What are the main issues you are concerned about?
What kind of society would you prefer to be living in?
What changes do you want our government to make?

These are the core questions of change and so make the Mandate a potentially powerful vehicle for change. However, before you write down your answers, it's important to do the next step.

Three

To clarify your thoughts, have conversations with friends and family about the Citizens' Mandate questions before answering them. This helps you get clearer and also spreads the message.

Four

Enter your Mandate, your 100 word answers to the three questions, on the website **citizensmandate.com** and click submit. This also adds your Mandate in to create a collective political voice. You can then opt to send it to your MP.

Five

Aim to spread the Mandate to at least three friends in three weeks, or better, spread it to a quarter of your most interested friends. Ask them to do the same and support them in doing this. As it spreads, the collective results are published monthly and sent to the media and politicians. The more you spread the word, the better.

How is the Mandate different to other campaigns?

It is based on open questions to get your personal views. It does not ask you closed questions and does not have a pre-set agenda. This makes it an open, inclusive, democratic, grassroots driven process.

The Mandate spreads by word-of-mouth through your personal network of friends; these are the strongest of social networks. It is a completely independent bottom-up process and is not spread by a central organisation through a funded campaign.

It has the potential to spread exponentially because it depends only on 'people power' and the whole project is self-funded through the sales of this book. This means you don't get pestered for donations.

It includes whatever concerns emerge from the Citizens' Mandate, so it covers the full range of issues which people consider important. This makes it a multi-issue rather than single issue campaign.

It aims at the biggest goal of all: to change the world by transforming our global systems in order to resolve our main issues and improve the wellbeing of people and the planet. Few other campaigns have this breadth and depth of scope.

How can the Citizens' Mandate spread?

The Mandate spreads primarily from person to person, whether face-to-face, by phone, on Zoom, or through other social media. It will also spread to different countries, and I cover that in Chapter Twelve.

As I mentioned, when I started talking with friends about the idea, the vast majority of the original group reported that their friends really liked the idea and wanted to know more about it. Many asked when the Citizens' Mandate website would be ready. Less than one in ten had any objections in the form of "Yes, but…", and the only one that came up repeatedly was that politicians didn't care anyway.

I don't happen to believe that. There is considerable evidence that the majority of MPs are interested to know what their constituents really think. They are tired of the usual media spin on issues. Knowing what their constituents really want enables them to position themselves better for a coming election. And most politicians do care about that.

I drilled down a bit further on how the conversations went. Typically, my friends said that the conversation had come about quite naturally when they were talking with their own friends. This happened when the topic veered towards any of the common areas of concern: climate change, the cost of living crisis, the ineffectiveness of politicians, hopelessness about the future, and so forth.

My friends would then mention their interest in the Citizens' Mandate, and the typical response was "What's that?" If it was a doom and gloom conversation, my friends might say they had come across this new thing that gave them more hope about the future, the

Citizens' Mandate for Change. Having reasons for hope seems to be a strong attractor, and most people like getting, and passing on, good news.

All very encouraging. The Citizens' Mandate clearly has the potential to be a 'viral meme', an idea and a behaviour that spreads. If it spreads enough, it could become that holy grail of change, an idea whose time has come. This led me to focus more on the specifics of spreading and reminded me of books I had read on the practicalities of creating successful social movements.

On creating social movements

For my money, one of the best books on this is *Rules for Revolutionaries – How Big Organising Can Change Everything*, by Becky Bond and Zack Exley. They give an insiders account of the massive movement they created, with virtually no funding, that came very close to succeeding with the Bernie Sanders presidential campaign in the USA.

A few key factors stood out. First and foremost, "the gold standard for making a difference is face-to-face conversations". The Mandate includes face-to-face conversations. It even improves on it because conversations with friends are more effective than conversations with voters who are strangers. In the Sanders campaign the volunteers were all talking with strangers.

The second factor was to "use volunteers to train volunteers". In our case, the equivalent of this is friends passing it on to friends, and explaining at the simplest level what the Mandate is and how it works. The website fleshes this out.

Third, "you win big when you ask big". The Mandate is asking for something big: a better world brought about by changing our systems of governance and economics so that they work better for people and better for the planet. This is a much bigger ask than just asking for a new politician.

Finally, "make your ask specific and do-able". So what, I wondered, could the best ask be? To spread the Mandate seemed too vague. To spread it to at least three friends was more specific, but it wouldn't necessarily go any further. However, to spread it to three friends who, in turn, spread it to three friends, gives it the potential to achieve exponential growth – the ultimate aim. Even better would be to ask them to spread it to a quarter or more of their friends. We'll see why this proportion is significant.

How fast could it grow?

However, this process lacked a timeframe. If each person spread it to only three friends in a year, it would be far too slow to be effective. To do it in a day, would simply be impractical. I had to make a decision, and quite arbitrarily I settled on three weeks. This seemed to me to be quite doable, even given a typical busy lifestyle. But would it be fast enough?

I did the maths and was pleasantly surprised. If the spread rate was only from you to three friends in three weeks, and they did the same, then we could, in principle, reach the entire population of the UK in under a year! If you spread it to a quarter of your friends it would be much faster. This is the power of exponential growth. And this is fast enough to change things before the next election. Clearly you would never reach the entire population, but to reach 25% seems possible, and we'll soon see why this is critically important.

In practice, we would probably achieve significant results much faster than this. If you include spread by social media, we're looking at a small number of months rather than a year. Add in the spread by high profile influencers, then just a month or two becomes feasible.

All this depends on the idea of the Citizens' Mandate gaining enough traction in the minds of individuals. And this, of course, means you, and all the other people it reaches; your friends and their friends.

There was only one way to find out, and that was to launch the project and see what happened.

Your part in practice

But what does all this mean in practice for you? The question here is: do you like the idea well enough that you are happy to talk about it? Most people seem to. But here, just for the minority who tend to dismiss anything new, I'd like to introduce a slightly challenging thought. Can you think of any better way of getting us out of the mess we're in? If you can, please spread it and change the world!

So, if you think the Citizens' Mandate has promise, the next question is: who do you know who is likely to be interested in this new idea? When you are with these people again, something in the conversation is likely to remind you of the Mandate, and that's the best time to mention it. Notice how interested they seem to be. If they are, tell them about it. If they are not, move on. That's it. It really is that simple.

If you are enthusiastic about the Mandate and you would like to do all you can to spread it, two aspects are important. The first is the number of people you talk with: the more the better. Start with those of your closest friends who you think are most likely to be interested. This will build your confidence and the satisfaction you get from your involvement. Gradually extend the people you talk with as promising situations occur.

The second aspect that makes a big difference is how soon you have conversations. Sooner is better, but don't bust a gut! Look for what works best for you. Above all, find creative ways of making it enjoyable. I've invited friends around to talk it through over a meal, and all were enthusiastic. One even said it was the most hopeful discussion about the future she had ever had! This was hard evidence for me that it can give people real hope.

Apart from conversations with friends, there are many other things you can do to spread the Mandate. Some people may want to offer talks to their local community groups, or in their workplace. Others may major on getting it out there on social media, and become super-spreaders. However, we are all different, and whatever you do, I think it's important that you only do what you find motivating and that you use the best approach for you. We'll look at more things you might want to do in the final chapter.

What are the tipping points for big social change?

If it does start spreading, the next question that comes up is, what proportion of the population would it need to reach to stand a good chance of actually changing things? Just as there are tipping points, bad ones, in the natural world, so there are tipping points, but good ones, in the world of social change.

In sociology, a tipping point is a time when a group rapidly and dramatically changes its behaviour by widely adopting a previously rare practice. Think how some of our behaviours changed so quickly in the Covid epidemic.

Damon Centola, in his book *Change: How to Make Big Things Happen* makes a strong case, based on his historical research, that around 25% is the tipping point for achieving significant social change. This has now become widely accepted. This means that for the Citizens' Mandate to be successful in achieving significant change, we need to reach 25% of the UK population, or around 12 million people of voting age. This is one reason why aiming to spread it to at least a quarter of your friends is a good idea.

There are other estimates. Malcolm Gladwell, in his book, *The Tipping Point: How Little Things can make a Big Difference* argues for a figure of 10%, or 5 million in the UK. His assumptions and his research base are different to Centola's. Gladwell places more emphasis on the role of high-profile key influencers, whom he calls connectors, and also on the role of spreaders in everyday social networks, whom he calls mavens. He points out that the idea has to be 'sticky' enough that people remember it and talk about it, and that the context has to be right. My informal research suggests that the idea of the Mandate is 'sticky' enough; and you decide when the context is right, because that's when it comes up in conversation.

A third estimate of the proportion of the population it takes to change things comes from the work of Erica Chenoweth, a political scientist at Harvard University. She observed that civil disobedience is the most powerful route to shaping politics, by a long way. Nonviolent campaigns are twice as likely to achieve their goals as violent campaigns. Although the exact dynamics depend on many factors, her historical research has shown that it takes around 3.5% of the population actively participating in protests out on the streets to ensure serious political change. That's around 1.8 million. Not that I'm suggesting getting out on the streets; it's simply not necessary.

That's three different estimates, so you can take your pick. I think they bode well for the Mandate. A few may think they should try and influence all their friends. I don't think so, it's better to aim at those who are likely to be interested. Ask yourself not only who is most likely to want to know about the Mandate, but also who is likely to be an influential spreader, both online, and in the face-to-face world.

Now, just suppose the Citizen's Mandate actually is an idea whose time has come, and it hits the social tipping points within a few months. What may happen then?

Chapter Four
Changing Our Political System

In this chapter I want to explore some of the changes which can take place if the Citizens' Mandate turns out to be a highly leveraged intervention, which you'll remember is a small thing which makes a big difference.

One characteristic of highly leveraged interventions in massively complex systems is that they trigger significant changes, and the changes they trigger are often of a highly unpredictable nature. Entirely new behaviours emerge at both the individual and the systemic level.

To the extent that we cannot predict the future, trying to do so is clearly a fool's errand, and I'm very mindful of this. However, in any of our previous social transformations, there have always been creative pioneers, explorers, and mapmakers. Their initial maps may often be wrong, but history shows that bad maps quickly get improved on.

This is the first chapter in which I'll look at the political system in more detail, so time for a bit of self-disclosure. I'm not aligned with any political party and my own views could be described as broadly 'progressive', but only in the sense of progress that genuinely works better for all. Wherever you see yourself on the political spectrum, I believe the Citizens' Mandate has to be inclusive of everybody to be effective. I cannot be 'unbiased', and I don't think any of us can, but I'll outline some possible scenarios for you to reflect on.

The purpose of this chapter is to imagine how a better future can come into being. I invite you to improve on these imaginings. Together, and with the Citizens' Mandate, I think we really do have the power to change things. I'm reminded of the quote from the famous anthropologist Margaret Mead:

"Never doubt that a small group of thoughtful, committed citizens can change the world; indeed, it's the only thing that ever has."

Well, if a small group can change the world, think what a big group can do, 25% of us, or more. We need to think big, so it's time to explore the realms of what becomes possible with the Citizens' Mandate at scale.

Possible political changes

We'll look here at how we can influence the political system and achieve the political power to achieve the changes that most of us want. The key time is in the run up to a general election. With the Mandate running at 25%, what becomes possible then?

Take first the landscape of different political parties. This will vary widely country to country, but here I'm only going to explore the possibilities in the UK. Unless the Conservative party abandon their entrenched position on the ideology of the neoliberal economic system, then based on current opinion polls, I suspect they are likely to take a massive hit and be out of the game.

Neoliberal capitalism

In brief, the neoliberal version of capitalism replaced the social democratic version of capitalism that ruled in the post-war period up to the elections of Thatcher and Regan. Social democratic capitalism, based on Keynesian economics, was the 'golden age' of capitalism. The famous British economist, John Maynard Keynes, published his economic thinking in his classic 1936 book, *The General Theory of Employment, Interest and Money.*

The golden age of capitalism was characterised by high growth rates, high employment, rising standards of living, a well-funded welfare state, free education at all levels, and a free health service that was the envy of the world. Income tax for the highest earners was around 90% and peaked at 99.25% during the war.

Since that time, from the days of Thatcher and Regan some 40 years ago until now, neoliberal capitalism has ruled much of the world. Neoliberal capitalism, as you'll remember, is an ideology, a system of ideas and beliefs, forming the basis of political and economic policy. The ideas of neoliberalism are based on the thinking of Friedrich Hayek, a British/Austrian economist, and others of the Mont Pelerin Society, founded in 1947. These ideas were massively funded and promoted by the rich and powerful. They still are.

The core ideas, at the most basic, are that nearly everything is best left to the market and government influence should be reduced to a minimum. As a result, neoliberal policies are in favour of a small state, privatisation, deregulation, free trade, low taxes and austerity. Is it a coincidence that these all favour the vested interests?

You could write a book on the devastating effects of this approach, and many have. Here are just three: *Profit Over People* by Noam Chomsky, *How Did We Get into this Mess* by George Monbiot, and *Globalization and Its Discontents* by Joseph Stiglitz. My one-liner summary would be this: with neoliberalism, the environment gets trashed and wealth concentrates in the hands of the few, causing ever growing inequality, which in turn amplifies most of the ills of society. Richard Wilkinson and Kate Pickett provided much evidence for the idea that inequalities amplify the ills of society in their well-known book *The Spirit Level.*

Other political parties

What of the Labour Party? At the moment, they could be described as neoliberal-lite. With the Citizens' Mandate at scale, it is possible that they will decide to run with this growing tide and change their policies significantly. Perhaps Labour would go for the most obvious alternative policy by investing in a massive GND. This could be paid for by increasing taxes on high earners, excess company profits, unearned income, wealth taxes, and so on, whilst tackling inequality head on.

Perhaps they may also include a Basic Citizens' Income. The Labour Party has significantly more potential for progressive policies than the Conservatives. They could make a change from neoliberalism to a much more ecological and egalitarian form of socialist capitalism with more in common with the post-war golden age of capitalism. Some new name may evolve for such a genuine alternative. Perhaps it will be called something like eco-socialism, eco-capitalism, or eco-social capitalism? Your guess is as good as mine.

What else may become possible?

Perhaps, with political turmoil caused by the growth of the Mandate, the conditions may emerge for a coalition of progressive parties aligning around the results of the Mandate, including minority parties such as the Liberal Democrats and the Green Party. Combined with tactical voting, this could open up the possibilities for even more significant change in the political landscape and bring a whole swathe of progressive policies.

Or a single party, such as the Green Party, could make a big jump forward because it is the party most likely to be aligned with the results of the Mandate. I'm reminded of a blind survey in which people were offered the policies of the different parties without knowing which party offered which policy. The most popular were the policies of the Green Party, so there is great potential there.

A new political party could emerge. There has been a growing wave of these in Europe over recent years: La République en Marche in France, Podemos in Spain, the Five Star Movement in Italy, and the Pirate Party in Sweden and 70 other countries.

Perhaps the Mandate will create a Citizens' Movement for Change, which might become a new political party. Who knows? If a new party did emerge in the UK, I believe it would be likely to encompass a more radical range of progressive policies than would be possible in the existing parties.

A new party could provide an opportunity for a political fresh start, with radical progressive policies. But whether the policies are relatively modest or radically transformative, you may be wondering how exactly we could achieve the political power to put these policies into effect?

How may we achieve political power?

We already know the numbers we are aiming at: anywhere between 3.5% and 25% of the population. Somewhere around this mark we start hitting real change. As I've said, what can't be predicted is exactly what this will look like. We know that when complex systems hit their tipping points, new patterns of behaviour, new phenomena, emerge, and the form they take is highly unpredictable. Let's explore some of the possible scenarios.

I've already mentioned one, the formation of a new political party. It might be called the Citizens' Movement for Change, or something else. If it adopts the policies that emerge from a huge popular Mandate, wins an election with them, and has a majority in Parliament, then that would be one way of achieving political power.

Another alternative is that a number of different new political parties might emerge. Division is the clear and present danger here. But what if, recognising the danger, they formed a coalition, either with each other, and/or with the more progressive of the existing parties? They would need to align with each other. How could this happen?

The Citizens' Mandate could be used as a tool for creating alignment. If the different parties wanted to combine forces, they could each ask all their members and supporters to complete the Citizens' Mandate and send it to them. It is then a relatively simple matter to merge the different Mandates and use this as the basis for agreeing what their shared policies would be.

Or another possibility could be the emergence of a massive campaign for independent MPs based on the results of the Mandate and the emergent policies. This would have the advantage of breaking the dominant power of political parties at a stroke.

Perhaps the thousands of different organisations for change would begin to align by using the Mandate process. This could involve any or all of the NGOs, charities, unions, and so on. Perhaps it may be called the Alliance for Change? As our government increasingly outlaws peaceful protest and, since 2019, puts concerned citizens in jail for peaceful protesting about the climate crisis, this will directly support these organisations looking for an alternative means of influence. It's not hard to imagine groups such as Extinction Rebellion taking up the Citizens' Mandate as a vehicle for change.

With the Mandate running at 25%, the entire mood of the country could shift in a more hopeful direction than we have seen for a long time. Think of the cultural shift of the sixties when, for a time, anything seemed possible. If you are not old enough to have been there, I'm afraid you'll just have to imagine it…

Any of the above may well emerge, or entirely new social phenomena, patterns of behaviour, or unexpected social inventions. This may all be hard to imagine from our present grim reality, but it's a territory of hope indeed. Then, at election time, bang! Change happens. Depending on what emerges from the Mandate, entirely new policy options could form. Even if they were on the modest side, the positive effects on society would be massive as we start on the journey to a society of fairness and justice for both people and the planet. But what if the pent-up forces for change were bigger than we can imagine from where we currently are?

What might the best-case scenario look like?

I want to start with a lesson from some 40 years ago when the last big change in economic thinking took place, from post-war Keynesian economics to the present neoliberal economics.

Here's a quote from Milton Friedman, the late University of Chicago professor who was perhaps the most influential economist of the last 50 years.

"Only a crisis – actual or perceived – produces real change. When that crisis occurs, the actions that are taken depend on the ideas that are lying around... Our basic function (is) to develop alternatives to existing policies, to keep them alive and available until the politically impossible becomes the politically inevitable."

We live in times of many ongoing crises; the perma-crisis, the poly-crisis, the meta-crisis, the great unravelling, or whatever you prefer to call it. Together, these crises create fertile ground for new thinking. What are some of the best ideas for political and economic change? Since many of these ideas are not yet widespread, thinking and talking about them is an important exercise in expanding our imagining as to what may be possible. I'd like to take the political possibilities first, before moving on to the economic possibilities.

Some of the best ideas for different political possibilities

It's time for more big thinking. And as an improbable start, here's a limbering up exercise. Do you know the age of the oldest complete Homo sapiens skeleton found in the UK? Cheddar Man, found in Gough's Cave in the Cheddar Gorge in Somerset. He lived in the Mesolithic, the stone age, 10,000 years ago.

Imagine living back then, then try this mental experiment. You go back in a time machine and have a conversation with him through a translator and you tell him about how you live. Do you think he would believe you? No, I don't think he would either.

Now try the opposite experiment. Go forward in the time machine 10,000 years, and let's assume you find someone to talk with. They try explaining their world to you. Do you think you would believe it? That's a difficult one because our beliefs limit what we think is possible. For this next exploration of democracy, you may want to temporarily suspend your disbelief, especially as we get to the outer limits of what's possible.

On democracy

If democracy means rule by the people, then representative democracy is an oxymoron, a contradiction in terms. It is rule by representative politicians, not rule by the people. What might an ideal democratic political system look like? Rule of the people, by the people, and for the people. And it would have to be 'rule' in a way that worked surprisingly well in practice.

It certainly wouldn't be a representative democracy based on political parties. This evolved to prevent democracy, that is rule by the people, and to keep as much power as possible in the hands of the few, which it does remarkably well. Voting for X or Y once every five years is about as little power as it's possible to have. No wonder we feel powerless! Jean-Jacques Rousseau, the 18th century philosopher, put it like this:

"The English people believes itself to be free; it is gravely mistaken; it is free only during the election of Members of Parliament; as soon as the Members are elected, the people is enslaved; it is nothing."

Why is government so dysfunctional?

You could write a book on this alone. And many have. The best one I know, and the most recent, is *How Westminster Works… and Why It Doesn't*, by Ian Dunt. It looks at how government in the UK actually works and is based on inside information from interviewing hundreds of key figures in the political system. If you want to understand how government in Westminster operates in practice, read this book. It explains how and why we end up with the dismal policies we have.

Most usefully, in the Epilogue to Dunt's book, he lists key changes which he considers would make the most difference. Since these apply directly mainly to the UK, I'll give just the briefest indication of what these are.

Improving our representative democracy

On the vote, he proposes proportional representation, outlined below. On the Members of Parliament, we could improve their performance by rationalising their workload. And we could also redesign the workings of Parliament itself to be much more effective and understandable to all. The centre of government is based in what is just a house, 10, Downing Street, which is simply not suitable. We could move it to somewhere like the Queen Elizabeth II Conference Hall in Westminster, with a Strategy Unit for long-term thinking, a Policy Unit, and a Delivery Unit.

Ministers have too much work, too little expertise available, and too little accountability. Their workload could be rationalised, and they could be held accountable to a select committee annually for a period of at least six years after they leave ministerial office. They would only be allowed to put people in charge of policy areas who have relevant experience and expertise.

The Treasury, which presides over our insanely complex tax system, also favours short-term financing over long-term. It could be redesigned for simplification of the tax system and improvement of sound long-term financing. It could also have its legislation scrutinised by the House of Lords, which it isn't at the moment. The Civil Service needs to be turned from a generalist organisation to an expert organisation with a managerial overlay, as so many investigations over decades have indicated.

In the Commons, perhaps the first priority is to bring government statutory instruments under control. They were originally intended to introduce legislation rapidly in an emergency but are now abused to push through whatever the government of the day wants.

The system should be overhauled based on the good work of the Hansard Society which has been trying diligently to fix the system for years. Many bills are pushed through without adequate scrutiny. Scrutiny could be more radical, inclusive, and comprehensive.

Scrutiny could include citizens' juries and select committees, both of which have a good track record.

Perhaps surprisingly, the House of Lords is in many ways one of the best functioning institutions in Westminster, but is not without its problems. Hereditary peers and bishops are an anachronism and the House of Lords itself wants them gone. Perhaps more seriously, the patronage power of Prime Ministers to appoint Lords is out of control with over 800 in the House of Lords. Lords' reforms should have two central goals: to prevent any party from controlling the chamber, and giving expert crossbench peers a decisive vote.

Finally, on the press, a major democratic deficit has been caused by the loss of most of our local papers. They used to report on the results of bad government policies, such as Universal Credit or the privatisation of the Probation Service, and the misery they caused on the ground. The least we could do would be to subsidise healthy local papers. We'll come back and look at the press's role in politics again.

Ian Dunt's many detailed proposals in his Epilogue are well and good, and would doubtless be a massive improvement, but I have a major concern and it can be summarised like this. If you take a basically lousy system and make it more efficient, you've just made a more efficiently lousy system...

There is a strong argument to be made that if we are to solve our main global problems in the time available, we need to jump to a much more effective form of democracy. Some have called it Democracy 2. We need to look beyond representative democracy. At the other end of the democratic spectrum, we have participatory and deliberative democracies, forms of direct democracy which also do away with political parties. One study, by Transparency International, revealed that political parties were perceived as being the most corrupt types of organisations of all.

Direct democracy involves representative members of the public directly in the political decision-making processes. Globally, there have been many successful examples of deliberative and participatory democratic innovations. Let's explore some first steps along this spectrum towards radically more effective forms of democracy. The following examples are from *Rebooting Democracy: A Citizen's Guide to Reinventing Politics* by Manuel Arriaga.

Some first steps towards better democracy

If we are to rebuild our democracy so that it is more, well, democratic, here are some core improvements.

Proportional representation

Here in the UK we currently have a first-past-the-post voting system. This is generally considered to be one of the worst kinds of voting system. The argument for it is that it is supposed to make a country more 'governable'. The larger and more mainstream parties get disproportionately more seats in Parliament compared to their numbers of voters and the smaller parties disproportionately less seats. This has serious negative implications.

It makes it very hard for new political parties to get seats in Parliament, thus favouring the status quo. It also means the main parties can, and do, get a working majority with a minority of the votes cast. The big parties therefore feel less threatened and less accountable. These factors contribute to the existence of a stale, self-assured political class that believes itself to be largely untouchable. Does this sound familiar?

Some form of proportional representation is used by most democracies, and in the developed countries, by the vast majority. Proportional representation refers to any type of electoral system in which the share of seats a party wins matches the share of votes it receives. All votes cast contribute to the final result and, put simply, it works better because it represents us better. No longer do the election results depend on only a few voters in a swing seat; everyone's vote counts. A recent survey in the UK (2023) found 45% were in favour of proportional representation with only 28% preferring first-past-the-post.

There are a variety of different proportional representation systems with each having different advantages and disadvantages. I will mention just one here, a rank voting system known as the single transferable vote (STV). It is successfully used to elect Parliaments in Ireland and Malta, and in Australia to elect the senate, as well as in other elections worldwide.

The basic idea is that when you vote, you put your candidates in rank order. When one of your candidates has no chance of being elected, you vote is transferred to your next favourite candidate. When a candidate has received enough votes to be elected, any surplus votes will be transferred to your next preferred candidate.

A form of proportional representation is common in many other countries. The main advantage is that the balance of MPs much more accurately represents the views of people in the country. It prevents one party dominating and leads to much more reasonable compromise in policies adopted and to better policies.

Fair political funding
Another major issue needing reform is campaign funding. The funding of parties and politicians by vested interests is a well-known problem in most countries, perhaps none more so than in the USA. The problem is how to insulate politics from the corrupting effects of the vast sums of private money used to buy political influence.

Politicians and parties need some funds for campaigning in the run-up to elections. If this funding is not to come from private sources, then it needs to come from the state. Some countries, like France, have already moved significantly in this direction.

One relatively straightforward way of doing this is to provide each voter with a 'democracy voucher' worth, say, £20. The voter can give this to any party or politician of their choosing, who can then cash it in to help fund their campaign.

To make this work, all other private contributions would need to be banned. To prevent money from the rich and powerful 'leaking in' there would also need to be a ceiling set on individual and party campaign spending.

This would effectively take the corrupting influence of wealth out of politics. It would also massively reduce the size of superficial advertising campaigns and increase the relative importance of informed debate.

Separating power from wealth

A much more important and wide-reaching issue than political funding is the part that wealth plays in politics generally. There is a sense in which democratic capitalism is a marriage of two quite different systems, politics and the economy.

To the extent that wealth confers political power, as it does in the UK, wealth corrupts democracy. Equally, to the extent that power confers wealth, it distorts the economy. Martin Wolf in his recent book *The Crisis of Democratic Capitalism* makes a compelling case for the crucial importance of maintaining a strong separation between power and wealth if we are to have an optimal form of democratic capitalism.

The practice of lobbying could be simply banned, but it would still be hard to prevent in practice. Perhaps a better idea would be to redesign the lobbying system to give all sectors of society an equal lobbying influence.

In addition, those with a net worth in excess of a few million pounds could be made ineligible for political service. The rotating door between politicians and high earners in the corporate world could be much more effectively regulated. A ten-year time limit would probably slow the rotating door down to a virtual standstill.

Checks between elections

Another significant problem for democracies is that after an election we lose control of the leading politicians. They can, and have, decided to start wars, commit to near-irreversible dismantling of welfare systems, and to introduce other massively unpopular policies. What can be done to curb such irresponsible behaviour between elections?

Some form of referendum perhaps? However, these can be a blunt instrument subject to press misinformation campaigns, and decidedly lacking in the reflective processes necessary to make well informed decisions. Consider Brexit. Enough said. Also, they would need to be subject to similar funding rules to elections themselves.

One promising option could be based on the Citizens' Initiative Review process used in the USA state of Oregon. They add in a deliberative layer before the referendum itself. A panel of 24 randomly chosen citizens deliberate for a number of days on the proposal. After interviewing advocates on both sides, calling whichever expert opinions they require, and extensive deliberation, they issue a public statement.

Written in plain English, and of not more than two or three pages, this statement documents the panel's key findings about the choice facing the electorate. It includes short statements by those who support and oppose the measure, the numbers of each, and any additional information the panel considers relevant.

The full statement is then sent out as a 'voter's pamphlet' to all voters before the referendum. Research shows that these reviews not only made citizens more knowledgeable about ballot measures, but they also substantially influenced the voting behaviour of those who read them.

The political impact of a referendum with a Citizens' Initiative Review could be further amplified by adding another option of removing a politician from office for deceiving the public or reversing the platform on which they were elected. In the referendum, voters would then have three different choices: to support the measure being challenged, to repeal the measure, or to repeal the measure and oust the politician proposing it.

Freeing the 'free press'

There is a strong argument to be made that what we consider to be the 'free press' isn't free at all. Almost all the print media are privately owned by billionaires. Only one newspaper in every 30 sold is owned independently. The vast majority of these billionaires' papers are both right-wing and neoliberal in their ideology. I do not think this is coincidental and it significantly biases people towards their agenda.

In the long term we need to remove the corrupting influence of massive wealth from the print media if we are to have a meaningful free press, just as we need to remove this same influence from politics itself. If we are to be able to legislate for a truly free press, we will first need to free our political system from the corrupting influence of excessive wealth. We'll look at how this may be done in practice later.

Overcoming political short-sightedness

A further problem with our political system is its short time horizon. The furthest it reaches is to the next election, a few years, and for senior politicians it seems to be mainly on the current news cycle, a few hours. This is partly due to the psychological bias we have towards focusing on the present and discounting the future. But short time horizons are also structurally built into our systems.

As we've seen, the economic system heavily discounts future profits against short-term profits, which makes it blind to long-term problems such as the climate crisis, or destroying the natural world on which we all depend. What can be done? With the political system we could build in a 'long now' function. This could be done with a large and representative 'Citizens' Assembly' which takes place every five years to create a vision of the kind of society most people want to be living in. Policy making could have a legal obligation to move in that direction.

This brings us to the role of Citizens' Assemblies, an example of participatory democracy. There is strong evidence that they do a better job of complex decision-making than politicians. If this is so, how could we incorporate them into the political system to best effect?

Sortition and Citizens' Assemblies

This is a fundamentally different kind of approach to the steps outlined above. The history goes back to Athenian democracy and a process called sortition, or selection by lot, that is, by lottery. It was the main process by which all political officials were chosen and was considered the best way to prevent abuses of power by politicians. The basic idea of choosing politicians by lottery is that you get a random, and therefore typical, selection of people who can best represent the common interest. It is very similar to how we still choose juries to this day.

This core idea from one of the earliest democratic societies has evolved considerably in recent years. The closest modern form is the Citizens' Assembly, or Citizens' Jury, as it is sometimes known. In the Citizens' Assembly, a group of people is chosen at random, typically from the list of jurors, to be representative of all ages, races, and classes. They are given a task, usually a decision to be made, and they meet once or a number of times. They are reasonably paid, given access to any expertise they want, and are provided with one or more skilled facilitators.

The research by James Fiskin, professor of communication at Stanford University, demonstrated the remarkable effectiveness of this process of deliberative democracy in outperforming politicians. This led to the acceptance of Citizens' Assemblies by political science and a rapid growth in using them to make difficult political decisions at all levels of government in the UK, and elsewhere. A good source of information on this is sortitionfoundation.org.

Two of the best-known examples were in Iceland to decide on their new constitution, and in Ireland to resolve the vexed issue of abortion.

The Citizens' Assembly, in a range of different forms and applications, can be used to cover many of the most important roles of political governance, giving us a fair, corruption free, and effective political system. A comprehensive account of this and how it could work in practice is the work of David van Reybrouck summarised in his classic book *Against Elections: The Case for Democracy.*

A recipe for good governance

In his book, van Reybrouck maps out how a multibody, sortition based, governance system would work in practice; it is a blueprint for better democracy based on sortition. This was originally devised and published in an academic periodical, *The Journal of Public Deliberation* (2013) by Terrill Bouricius, a researcher with twenty years' experience as a politician.

Bouricius's legislative assemblies

With a prospective European Parliament in view, he balanced theory and practice with six different legislative assemblies each having a different role. Here's a brief outline.

An Agenda Council

This compiles the agenda and chooses the topics for legislation. Chosen by lot from volunteers, the Agenda Council comprises some 200 to 400 people, possibly in sub-committees. They would work with full-time salaries for three years, with one-third replaced every year.

Interest Panels

These would then choose topic-related legislation. There would be an unlimited number of panels, each made up of 12 people drawn by lot from volunteers who would assemble as often as needed to meet a deadline and would be unpaid.

Review Panels

The Review Panels then compile the legislation according to the input of Interest Panels and experts. 150 people, drawn by lot from volunteers, are allocated to different panels to deal with each piece of proposed legislation. This is full-time salaried work for three years with one-third replaced every year.

A Policy Jury

This then votes on each piece of legislation by secret ballot after public presentations. Each Policy Jury is made up of 400 people drawn by lot from the entire adult population and is compulsory, much like jury service. A new jury is called for each piece of legislation and typically lasts for a number of days. It listens to the cases for and against a piece of proposed legislation before voting. Each jury member is paid a generous daily rate plus expenses.

The Policy Jury is the central part of this whole process and makes the key legislation decisions. It is worth emphasising that, in contrast to our present system, there is no party discipline, no back scratching, no pressure, no tactical voting, no political haggling, no group pressures, and most importantly, no corruption and no lobbying.

In politics, this combination of features is a veritable holy grail. Whatever system we adopt, if it does not incorporate these features we will surely fail in transforming the political system. These features are also the main reasons why Citizens' Assemblies work so well in practice.

A Rules Council

This is an additional part of Bouricius's proposal. This council decides on the rules and procedures of all legislative work. It is made up of 50 people drawn by lot from volunteers, including those who have previously worked in the other legislative assemblies. They are salaried full-timers taken on for three years with one-third replaced every year. An important feature is that, through the Rules Council, the whole process becomes a self-evolving system. One nice detail is that the Rules Council would be forbidden from granting more power to itself.

An Oversight Council

This regulates the legislative process and deals with complaints. Around 20 people are chosen by lot from volunteers, including those who have served on the other legislative assemblies. Again, they are salaried full-timers taken on for three years with one-third replaced every year.

How this could all work makes compelling reading and would be a giant leap in the direction of an ideal democratic political system.

Other forms of more direct democracy

William Gibson, an award-winning science fiction author, said something to the effect that the future is already here, it's just not very evenly distributed. Let's take a look at some new aspects of democracy which are already with us. There are many democratic innovations spreading throughout the world and one of these is participatory budgeting.

Participatory budgeting

The first full example of participatory budgeting took place in Porto Alegre in Brazil in the late eighties, and since then the practice has spread widely. Participatory budgeting can work in a similar way to Citizens' Assemblies but to decide all or part of a budget. It can also be used to decide all or part of a budget with a mass of ordinary people voting. Participatory budgeting can be used at every level from the municipal to the national. Perhaps more importantly, it could also be used at the global level.

Liquid democracy

Another innovation is 'liquid democracy'. This is a form of delegative democracy in which people engage in decision-making, usually online, through direct participation and dynamic representation which uses elements of both direct and representative democracy. Voters have the right to vote directly on issues, but can also delegate their vote to someone who will vote on their behalf. Any individual may be delegated votes from others, and may in turn delegate their vote to others. In both cases, this can include votes which they have been delegated by others, resulting in 'meta-delegation'.

Online democracy

Taiwan, with 23 million people, leads the world in the development of online democracy. Let's have a look at what there is to learn from this exemplar of best practice.

The book *Citizens* by Jon Alexander gives an outline. As an aside, his book is based on the idea of our identity shifting from being subjects, to consumers, and on now to being citizens. This shift in identity towards citizens is one reason why I chose the Citizens' Mandate for Change as the name of this project.

In *Citizens*, Alexander offers many examples of citizens taking different forms of democratic action across different countries. There is much best practice to learn from. But in Taiwan, we have probably the most evolved example of online democratic involvement and citizen government. How did it begin?

In 2011, a group of democratically motivated programmers and developers began to organise. They set out to 'fork' the government by setting up parallel websites to those of the government. They called themselves Gov Zero after replacing the letter 'o' in gov.tw with the number '0'. They scraped together whatever relevant information they could get from the government websites and made it accessible and visually engaging.

Their first project was a citizen audit system that allowed anyone to grade and comment on different aspects of the government budget. From a small base, their projects grew rapidly. In 2014 they took on the government over an unpopular trade deal with China.

They occupied Parliament, and discussion groups were broadcast first online, and then in national media. Gov Zero won.

Unusually, the Speaker of the House took a position that validated the protest. On getting an agreement to re-examine the trade deal, the protestors vacated Parliament. In the subsequent local elections politicians were elected who stood up for the protesters. Senior government ministers reached out to the leader of Gov Zero, Audrey Tang, and formed an alliance. They worked together to bring the Gov Zero approach into the processes of government.

By the end of 2015, that led to the creation of a participatory policy-making platform called vTaiwan built on open-source software called pol.is. They first demonstrated its effectiveness by crowdsourcing what turned out to be the world's most successful regulatory framework for Uber.

Audrey Tang was appointed to power to become a 'channel' to allow greater combinations of strength and intelligence to come together online. As she said:

"We don't care much about whether the people trust the government or not, but we care a lot about the government trusting its people."

Taiwan rose to the top of global rankings for open government and successfully ran extensive participatory budgeting processes. When Covid showed up, Taiwan used its crowdsourced open governance platforms to build a very effective response based on the belief that its people were intelligent, capable, and responsible.

Taiwan had its first confirmed case of Covid on 21st January 2020. At the end of April 2021, they had recorded only nine deaths and under 1,000 Covid infections. There was no lockdown, and their economy was growing at its fastest rate in seven years. They had the most effective Covid policies on the planet. New Zealand's outstanding response to Covid was based on Taiwan's. Compare that to what happened in the States or here in the UK. This level of outstanding national performance is what citizen government makes possible.

The institutions of this kind of government act as cooperative platforms with the citizenry in a way that Tang describes as fast, fun, and fair. They surface the best suggestions and then move them rapidly to the best practical implementations. And they do this by constant iteration; constantly repeating and improving processes until they work well.

This is not so much government as governance. And it is a far cry from how many Parliaments and government institutions currently work. I find it striking that we take for granted regular upgrades to our IT systems, but significant upgrades to our government systems are simply not on the agenda. There hasn't been such an upgrade to our systems of government within living memory; perhaps a serious one is overdue...

A synthesis of democratic improvements

We've looked at a range of different democratic innovations including Terrill Bouricius's outline for improving the workings of a parliamentary system, different forms of more direct democracy, and Taiwan's world-leading version of online participatory democracy. Imagine combining all these improvements. We could have a governance system well able to deal with the challenges we face.

Used together, these different democratic innovations would create something very close to rule of the people, by the people, and for the people. It could work surprisingly well in practice. All the component parts have been well tried and tested. They have simply not all been put together at the national level yet. The reason is that the vested interests, particularly in the form of the media, are usually vehemently opposed to such notions. And for obvious reasons; the vested interests would be rapidly displaced from power and wealth.

So, we can imagine how to create a completely different political system which could work highly effectively to deliver the kinds of new policies we need. What might these policies be?

New political policies and the Green New Deal

These policies will need to be progressive, and they would need to include the adoption of some form of the GND. That would be good news. The idea of a GND originated in the UK in 2008 from a report released by the Green New Deal Group and published by the New Economics Foundation. It is loosely based on a fusion of the original New Deal and a range of solutions to the financial and environmental problems we currently face.

President Roosevelt's successful New Deal in the USA in the 1930s addressed the problems of the great depression and mass unemployment. It involved big public spending on a series of programs and public works projects to kick-start the economy.

The Green part of the GND adds to the old New Deal the solutions to the current problems that we face. These include policy proposals to tackle the climate crisis and the other environmental problems as well as financial inequality, the root cause of our current cost of living crisis.

The GND became better known when Alexandria Ocasio-Cortez and Ed Markey introduced a resolution for it to the United States Congress in 2019. It was a comprehensive plan to achieve five major goals over a ten-year mobilisation. They were to:

- Reach net zero greenhouse gas emissions through a fair and just transition
- Create millions of well-paid jobs and economic security for all
- Invest in infrastructure and industry to sustainably meet the 21st century challenges
- Promote justice and equity by preventing oppression of all vulnerable communities

- Create a sustainable environment for all through clean air and water, climate and community resilience, healthy food, and access to nature

There is a wide range of GND proposals from the relatively business-as-usual ones through to those involving radical redesign of our economic and other systems. We will come back to look at these again, and other options too.

A spectrum of possibilities

Clearly, there is a wide spectrum of political possibilities. At one end are relatively small tweaks to the existing system which could have a significant impact. An example of this would be the introduction of proportional representation which would break us out of the first-past-the-post system.

At the other end of the spectrum would be a radical redesign of the entire structure of the formal governance system, which includes the executive, the legislature, and the judiciary. Government is currently dominated by government departments running top down power hierarchies. You could argue that the core design principles here haven't changed much since the days of the Roman Army.

There is a serious question as to how fit for purpose the present governance system is, especially with levels of trust in government being at an all-time low. If we were to start again, where else might we look for more inspiration?

Governance at heart is about organisation and communication in complex systems. Driven in large part by the needs of World War Two a new science evolved, cybernetics, the science of organisation, a forerunner of systems thinking. Let's take a look at this next.

Chapter Five
Governance Systems for a World Which Works

Norbert Weiner, one of main developers of cybernetics, and author of the book *Cybernetics* (1948), defined the field back then as "The science of control and communication in the animal and the machine"; it came to be pretty much about organisation and communication in complex systems, both natural and man-made. What does this have to offer that is of practical value in governance?

One of the leading developers of cybernetics was Stafford Beer, an international consultant in the sciences of management and effective organisation, who pioneered the field of management cybernetics. His life work was in developing a model of thinking and practice for what worked best in organisations. He called it the Viable Systems Model (VSM). Stafford Beer worked in global governance with the UN, with other international bodies, with major corporations, and with the governments across the world. He was a larger than life figure.

I wondered whether to include his VSM. After all, at the level of the organisation, or the nation state, we can look for the best practice examples to learn from. However, best practice does not help when it comes to designing a new kind of organisation, or a new kind of nation state. And when it comes to international governance, there are no other forms of international governance to learn from.

Stafford Beer's Viable Systems Model

I think the VSM is important and foundational in looking to the future beyond best practice examples. It provides a blueprint for designing as yet unimagined future forms of organisation, from small organisations, right through to a system of international global governance. It also offers a framework for diagnosing the problems of any existing organisation. By superimposing the VSM over the actual structure of any organisation, you can see the structural or systemic weaknesses of that organisation.

The VSM is based on living organisms, and maps out the main structural elements and linkages, or feedback loops, by which complex organisms and organisations maintain their viability. To be viable is to be capable of working successfully and maintaining itself in the face of variety. Stafford outlined the VSM in many of his books, but perhaps of greatest relevance to our present predicament is *Platform for Change*. Be warned, this is not an easy read, even though inspiring. His earlier book *Designing Freedom* is perhaps an easier starting place.

Here is a brief outline. The VSM is made up of five core elements, or systems, that are necessary and sufficient for any organisation to maintain itself and its viability in the face of a complex and ever-changing world.

One of the more profound aspects of the VSM is that it is a recursive system. It is rather like a series of nested Russian dolls. The system both contains itself and is contained within itself. That is, each system of the VSM is made up of VSMs one level down, and each VSM is itself a subsystem of a VSM one level up. You can focus up or down on the level of interest to you.

System One

This focuses on the fundamental operations that the organisation does in providing a service or a product. It has to sense what is wanted, and have the capability of providing it. There are typically many different kinds of System One in an organisation. For example, if you are a widget manufacturer, to produce a widget you need to source the components, manufacture widgets, and sell them. These are three quite different System One operations.

System Two

This is the system that coordinates the activities of System One. In the example above, it is the coordination of the sourcing, manufacturing, and selling of your widget. System Two is about how the left hand knows what the right hand is doing, and it coordinates accordingly.

System Three

This is the system that manages and coordinates all of the above, the management of everything within the organisation. It can be thought of as managing in the 'here and now'. In our example it is all the internal processes of managing or running the business.

System Four

The purpose of this system is to look outside the organisation at the surrounding world as it is in the present, as well as how it may be different in the future. In other words, it looks at the present and possible future environments in which the business operates, or may operate. Think of this as attempting to manage the business in its present and future environments by sensing the 'there and then'.

System Five

Here the function is to balance the resource demands of System Three, the 'here and now' management, with those of System Four, the 'there and then' management. If either dominates, the business will crash either in the now, or in the future. This is also the level at which organisational policy is made.

As I mentioned, one of the main strengths of the VSM is that you can map this blueprint onto any existing organisation and see the system's structural weak spots. Just one example here, Kodak, who used to dominate photography and who first developed digital photography, was weak in the 'there and then' department. Kodak died.

Big companies used to have a lifespan of 60 years. As the rate of change speeds up, this is currently 18 years and falling. The VSM has much to offer in the future-proofing of organisations. You can also use the VSM as a blueprint for designing fit for purpose organisations from scratch.

On a personal level, when working in organisational change I used many different skills and models from psychology and systems thinking. I found the VSM to be one of the most useful in practice.

All very well, you may say, but what has this to do with governance? Well, governance is a system of organisations that provide services to society, so the VSM can be applied directly.

The VSM in governance

Of all the work Stafford did for governments, one of the most relevant to us was an unusual project that emerged in Chile. Back in 1970, Salvador Allende, the president, was the only person to have been elected by a democracy on a basically Marxist platform. However, he was not remotely a traditional Marxist. He was against traditional capitalism and was looking for the social benefits Marx wanted, but without all the communist baggage. As Karl Marx famously said before writing *The Communist Manifesto*:

"The philosophers have hitherto only interpreted the world in various ways. The point, however, is to change it."

Salvador Allende sought out Stafford Beer. They were aligned in their social goals and put together the Chilean road to socialism; this was a project to apply Stafford's VSM thinking to the Chilean economy. In my opinion it was perhaps the single most interesting and significant political and economic experiment of the twentieth century. Few people have heard of it. I think it is worth outlining here because it points the way to a different and more effective form of governance.

The VSM in Allende's Chile

Stafford's mission was to install a kind of nervous system for the Chilean social and economic system. Starting in 1973, he and his team designed and delivered a hypermodern information system that would make this possible and bring socialism into the computer age. The system he devised was called Cybersyn (a contraction of cybernetic synergy) and the Central Operations Room looked like something out of Star Trek.

Back in the seventies computers were primitive, yet he succeeded in designing a system that was capable of organising up to a third of the Chilean economy in close to real time, and to do it so effectively that it could potentially outperform a traditional capitalist economy. In a number of ways, it prefigured important aspects of our big-data modern internet world. Yet it was egalitarian in design, supported worker participation, and devolved control down throughout the system.

Stafford's views on money were ahead of their time. He thought of money as a constraint, rather than as a goal. He believed the goal of human organisations should be wellbeing, and that his cybernetic systems would have human wellbeing as their ultimate goal. The word he preferred for this was eudemony, from the Greek 'eu' meaning good, and 'demos' meaning people. The closest we can get to this in English is a sense of thriving or flourishing wellbeing. As the ultimate measure, or metric, it is about as good as it gets. However, as it is a little-known term, I will stay with wellbeing.

As a side aspect of the project, Stafford developed a simple device to measure wellbeing, an algedonic meter, from the Greek 'algos', pain and 'hedone', pleasure. Installed in peoples' homes and workplaces, you changed the dial to reflect how you were feeling. There were problems with it and it wasn't deployed at scale, but it was an interesting idea.

The USA did not approve of Allende's Chilean socialist experiment. It was socialist after all. There was a major CIA attempt to block Salvador Allende's election in 1970, with subsequent economic embargoes intended to destabilise him. The USA encouraged a military coup, but it is disputed whether they directly financed it. The subsequent military coup put Pinochet in power in 1975. Salvador Allende shot himself. Stafford lost dear friends, but, by chance, was in London at the time and survived. The rest is sad history. Project Cybersyn had lasted just 16 months. Much later, Colin Powell as Secretary of State said, "It is not a part of American history that we're proud of."

We can only wonder what might have been. However, it did demonstrate the considerable potential of the VSM deployed at the level of the nation state. This may be an idea whose time is coming, and we will return to it later.

Looking to exemplars

A quite different approach for improving how any country is run is to look for the best examples to be found in the other 195 or so countries of the world. Looking for best practice exemplars is a good general strategy for improving things based on not reinventing wheels, that is, not wasting time trying to invent something that somebody has already invented. It is much underused.

In fancier language, the strategy involves seeking the best outlier and doing a contrastive analysis of the differences between the way they do something and the way you do it. You then change the way you do it to incorporate the key elements of how they do it; it will typically need tailoring to suit local circumstances. You can apply this learning and development strategy at any level from the individual, to the organisation, to the nation state.

Which nation is most worth looking at as an exemplar?

There are many different indices of national wellbeing. They each give different weightings to different aspects of life such as income level, life expectancy, and so forth. One that I particularly like is based on subjective wellbeing: The World Happiness Report. Finland gets top place, and also scores well in many other indices. So, how do the Finns achieve this? What exactly are they doing differently?

Danny Dorling and Annika Koljonen have researched this and summarise the results in *Finntopia – What we can Learn from the World's Happiest Country*. Clearly, the Finns are doing quite a lot of things right because they also rank at or near the top in: equality, honest government, education, safety, stability, human capital, trust in the police, and 96 other areas. Eighty years ago, none of this was true. What happened?

At its simplest, the Finns have prioritised equality and invested in people and the welfare state far more than most countries. To pay for this massive social investment they have chosen to increase taxation. In 2017, their tax-to-GDP ratio was 43.3% compared to 33.3% in Britain; and they tax higher incomes more. This, of course, flies in the face of neoliberal orthodoxy, which believes higher taxes make things worse.

Thomas Piketty's *Capital in the Twenty-First Century* looked at the causes of inequality and proposed higher taxes on income and wealth as the best solution. The example of Finland backs this up, and we will come back to it.

Neoliberalism argues that state expenditure is not as effective as the so-called free market, and so favours a small state. The Finnish success story provides clear and compelling evidence that the opposite is true.

Higher taxes, especially for the wealthiest and the highest earners, and a bigger state investing more in the social capital of its people, is clearly a central part of what works best.

Putting it all together

Combining Finland's world-leading example with the earlier outline of Bouricius's parliamentary system based on Citizens' Assemblies, and Stafford's VSM thinking about how best to organise organisations, we can begin to imagine something like the following.

A sortition based parliamentary system, based on Terrill Bouricius's six different legislative assemblies, would be effective at introducing new legislation to enact the wishes of the Citizens' Mandate for Change as expressed in the policies that effectively won the election.

This legislation would enable government departments to be reorganised to function more on the lines of viable systems. Departments would act more like true public services, driven democratically from the bottom up, and they would be better at meeting people's real needs. This would work better than the present top-down command and control system driven by the short-term interests of ministers and lobbyists funded by the rich and powerful.

This new kind of state, now functioning better at meeting people's needs for education, health, welfare, as well as the needs of our living environment, would grow in size. This growth would be financed by increased taxation of the wealthy.

Broadly, this all adds up to a GND, outlined earlier. And the effect of this would be a society much more capable of delivering wellbeing for people and the environment.

So far, this all seems both desirable and practical, but it hasn't happened. Why not?

What are the forces locking us into the status quo?

I want to introduce here the concept of consensus reality. Consensus reality is simply what is generally agreed by society. We met this earlier on a smaller scale in the form of groupthink. We are social animals and will usually go along with what we believe others think. However, what we think others think, we often get wrong.

Next concept: the myth of the consensus reality. This is the idea that societies often have mistaken beliefs about reality. 2,600 years ago, the belief that the Earth was flat was universal. 300 years ago, the belief that women were inferior to men was the norm.

Now the belief that economic growth is good, and that there are no limits to economic growth on Earth is still pretty much the norm, especially in neoliberal economic and political circles. Almost all news items will refer to economic growth as good. This is a consensus reality, and it is also a myth.

The print and broadcast media

Where do our consensus realities come from? A main source, and probably the main source, is the print and broadcast media. Why do we behave as though the climate crisis is not a problem when no less than the Secretary General of the UN says that with business-as-usual we are doomed?

Much of the time, most of the media obsesses over issues of mind-numbing triviality. They seldom mention the climate crisis. Issues of existential importance are largely ignored, and the fundamental causes are simply not aired; this is denialism in practice. It is as if the media collectively is behaving as a weapon of mass distraction. Why?

George Monbiot, in a recent article in the Guardian, summarised the answer eloquently:

"The reason is not difficult to discern. Most of the media are owned by corporations or billionaires, who have a financial interest in sustaining business as usual. If governments acted to prevent the collapse of Earth systems, business models would have to change drastically, and these changes would disfavour legacy industries and their investments. To keep the proprietors, shareholders and advertisers happy – or, in the case of public sector broadcasters, to keep the government off their backs – the most important topics are neglected."

The TV media, including the BBC, seem to mainly follow the print media, who appear to largely set the daily news agenda. This has a dominant influence on consensus reality, on what the agenda is, and what are, and are not, considered to be the important issues. Importantly, the media also sets many of our background assumptions, such as growth is good.

Here in the UK, one of the few main newspapers not owned by a billionaire, or a billionaire dominated corporation, is The Guardian. The Guardian and the Observer are owned by an independent trust, The Scott Trust, and its purpose is to "secure the financial and editorial independence of the Guardian in perpetuity and to safeguard the journalistic freedom and liberal values of The Guardian free from commercial or political interference." Perhaps this is why it carries more challenging and progressive news items.

However, its circulation, and therefore its influence, is tiny in comparison to the billionaire-owned press. The Guardian sells around 110,000 copies daily compared to around 3,380,000 for the combined right-wing press, just 1 in 30 of newspapers sold.

On the bias of the overwhelming mass of the print media, there was an interesting piece of research which showed that, as a result of media coverage of significant areas, readers ended up worse informed than if they had read nothing!

So it seems that the media, as the primary mouthpiece of vested interests, is what is stopping us from changing to systems that work better for all. What happens if and when the Citizens' Mandate is taken up by an exponentially growing number of people?

How will the media respond to the Citizens' Mandate?

The Mandate will, of course, be ignored by the right-wing media at first. But as it scales, this strategy will no longer work. My guess is that after ignoring it, the media will dismiss it as irrelevant. Next, they will ridicule it. After that, the media will viciously attack it, and you can see why. As the Mandate continues to grow, the attacks will be ramped up, perhaps along these lines: it won't work, it's misguided, it's a lefty lunacy, it's woke gone mad, it's a socialist plot, it's an environmentalist plot, it's a communist plot, it'll destroy our democracy, it's dangerous, it should be made illegal, and so on.

So, what is our best line of response? Here are a few thoughts. First, bad publicity is better than no publicity. Second, at the 10-20% level, pretty much everybody will know others in their social network who have used the Mandate to make their voice heard. Are these people going to believe what the papers are saying, or what their friends and family are saying? Third, pushing a view that such a large number of us are opposed to, the media may well create an equal and opposite resistance to themselves. This may even amplify the power of the Mandate.

The vested interests will start paying enormous sums of money to attack the Citizens' Mandate with social media disinformation. However, the social media will know that this is happening and will probably actively engage with it. All of this will probably make the issues at stake, our future, really come to the fore and everyone will be talking about it.

If everybody is talking about it, this looks remarkably like what happens when a major social transformation is taking place. Perhaps this is all a necessary part of what has to happen for significant change to come about.

We've looked at a range of promising options for change to the political system so that it becomes more fit for purpose. Time now to look at some of the most promising options for change in the economic system. Because, of course, the aim of changing the political system is to change the economic system in which we are trapped.

Chapter Six
Changing Our Economic Systems

Economics can seem mind-numbingly boring, and I've tried to avoid this. In this chapter we'll be taking an overview of some of its main features. It's important to have a broad understanding of these if we are to succeed in transforming our dangerously dysfunctional economy to the kind of economic system which will be necessary for a better future.

Before looking at the formal economy itself, it's important to remember that a lot of the real work of the world takes place outside the formal economy. I'm thinking here of the unpaid work of raising children, of caring for those with health problems, of all the work done by volunteers in so many good causes, and so on. I've read estimates that up to a third of all work done is unpaid.

Then there is the black economy, and undeclared work for cash. Italy is one of the few countries to estimate this and include it in its total of goods and services. Italy estimates the size of the black economy at about a fifth of the total. Taken together with unpaid work, then maybe half of all work exists outside the formal economy.

If we look at wealth, rather than work, about 10% of all wealth exists in tax havens. This too is effectively outside of the economy.

Who, or what, are the main players in the economy? Some of the contenders here would be the market, the state, businesses, the commons, households, and you, the individual. In many ways the commons are one of the most interesting of these.

The Commons

The commons, originating from the common land of medieval England, are the cultural and natural resources accessible to members of society. Commons can also be understood as natural resources that groups of people, communities or user-groups, manage for mutual benefit.

The commons became a lot less common as the wealthy enclosed them. The Enclosure Acts of Parliament from the 17th century onwards removed some seven million acres, a fifth of England, from common ownership. This was the land to which people had common rights to grazing, food, fuel and so on.

Much later, the commons got a poor reputation in part as a result of a famous paper, the Tragedy of the Commons, published by the ecologist Garrett Hardin in 1968. This made a case that commons would tend to be exploited until they were exhausted.

The Nobel Prize winning economist, Elinor Ostrom, in her 2015 book Governing the Commons, critiqued the flaws in Hardin's thinking and outlined the eight principles for successful governance of commons based on her research of best practice examples. The conclusion of her critique is that we know how to make the commons, or common ownership, work.

In the global transformation that is needed, we may well see a resurgence in new forms of commons, as we saw with Wikipedia. Here are just a couple of examples. The digital commons may be partly or wholly reclaimed from the digital elite. Given the importance of the print media in determining the consensus reality, they may also be reclaimed as a commons.

Professor of Economics, Guy Standing, in his 2019 book *The Plunder of the Commons – A Manifesto for Sharing Public Wealth* gives a good overview and many more examples of what is possible with rejuvenated commons.

Apart from reclaiming much of the media, we could reclaim the national infrastructures and services which have been privatised, and we could go further by reclaiming the financial systems themselves as commons. In short, we may see a major move from private to common ownership. But enough speculation, and back now to looking at what is normally thought of as 'the economy'.

The monetary system and the fiscal system

The economic system is made up of two distinct subsystems, the monetary system and the fiscal system.

Monetary policy concerns the quantity of money and credit in the economy and is governed by the central national bank. In the UK this is the Bank of England. Fiscal policy concerns taxation and spending and is governed by the political decisions of the government.

We will explore the kinds of change we need in each of these. The difference between the monetary and the financial systems explains why the national economy is a completely different kind of beast to the household economy. Many of the assumptions we have, based on the workings of our household economies, simply do not apply at the level of the national economy. We'll come back to this important point.

Microeconomics and macroeconomics

Within the fiscal part of the financial system, economics is divided into two quite different categories: microeconomics and macroeconomics.

Microeconomics is the study of individual and business decisions, focussing on supply and demand, and is a bottom-up approach. Macroeconomics looks at the big financial decisions of countries, focuses on the financial economy as a whole, and is a top-down approach.

There are, have been, and no doubt will be, many different types of economic systems. Let's focus on the economic system we have had for the last 40 years.

We looked earlier at the fundamental causes of climate change, our other main environmental problems, inequality, and the major social ills we face. The underlying cause of all these is the present economic system, the rather extreme form of market capitalism, known as neoliberal economics.

Neoliberal economics

We've looked at this before, but what exactly is neoliberal economics? It is the orthodox model of economics that has been dominant for most or all of our lifetimes. At heart it is an ideology, a belief system, that greater economic and social progress can be made when government participation in the economy is minimised: less government regulation, less government spending and taxes, and less government control of the economy. This means greater freedom for the financial system and the wealthy.

Warren Buffet, one of the world's richest men, famously said in 2006:

"There's class warfare alright. But it's my class, the rich class that are making war, and we are winning."

As an aside, and to be fair to him, he also said it was wrong that he paid a lower proportion of his income in tax than anyone else in his office.

There's a saying in systems thinking: "A system is what a system does." The neoliberal economic system concentrates wealth and power in the hands of the few. And it is very good at it. One of the main unintended consequences of this includes ramping up inequality and all the negative social consequences which, if continued, will lead to social breakdown. The other main unintended consequence is the enormous range of damage to the natural world on which we all depend. Ever increasing financial inequality and damage to our ecosystems will lead to the collapse of civilisation at some point in the not too distant future. It usually has in previous civilisations.

The primary measure of the success of the neoliberal economic system is economic growth. This is measured by Gross Domestic Product (GDP), the total value of all goods and services. It is one of the worst measures of economic success. As the present economic system grows, multiple damage grows.

This system is rather like a cancer on the face of the Earth. This is so because neoliberal economics takes no account of two key externalities, the natural world of our planet, and the social world of human society. To quote from two of the past leaders of neoliberal economics:

Ronald Regan

"There are no great limits to growth…"

And Margaret Thatcher

"… there's no such thing as society."

According to some estimates, if all the externalities were fully costed in, most economic growth would actually be uneconomic; it costs more than it delivers. This is a remarkable state of affairs and bears repeating. Most economic activity is uneconomic. However, if the full environmental and social costs of economic activity were factored in, the economic system would have to behave very differently. We would then have an economic, rather than an uneconomic, economy.

Towards more ecologically sound economic systems

Instead of an extractive economic system, we need a regenerative one; one that regenerates the quality of life for human societies and for the natural world. What might this look like?

There are many different schools of economics, such as ecological economics which has been growing since the eighties. These different schools of economics have different assumptions. Ecological economics assumes that the economic system is embedded in a social system, which in turn is embedded in an environmental system; it takes account of the externalities.

This is in marked contrast to neoliberal economics which assumes economics is separate from its effects on the rest of the world. Some of the main schools of ecological economics include:

- Doughnut Economics
- Steady-state Economics
- De-growth
- The Circular Economy
- The Green Economy

They sound promising. Let's look at some of these ideas in more depth.

Kate Raworth's Economic Doughnut

First up, and one of the best known, is an idea that was developed by the University of Oxford economist Kate Raworth, called Doughnut Economics. There's an image, on page 111, which summarises it and was made famous by her 2017 book, *Doughnut Economics: Seven Ways to Think Like a 21st-Century Economist*.

She proposed the diagram to show the performance of an economy measured by the extent to which it meets the needs of people without overshooting the Earth's ecological limits. One of her aims was to set new goals for a viable economy. An economy is considered to be prosperous when all twelve social foundations are met without overshooting any of the nine ecological planetary boundaries. This situation is represented by the area between the two rings, which she calls the safe and just space for humanity.

The economic doughnut meets the explicit aims of the new economic system we need. It combines the safety of the environmental ceiling of the nine planetary boundaries with the social foundation of the twelve human needs which are necessary to provide for our wellbeing.

Being visual, it is intuitively easy to understand. It could also be used as a dashboard of the 21 main measures which we need to be paying the greatest attention to. You can imagine it being plugged into Stafford Beer's main control room as we navigate spaceship Earth, its living world and all its people into a safe and just future.

I can't help but notice that the biggest of our unmet social needs is for a political voice. I don't need to spell out how the Citizens' Mandate at scale would satisfy this need, and in turn bring pressure to bear on improving the other social foundations and the nine planetary boundaries.

The Doughnut of social and planetary boundaries

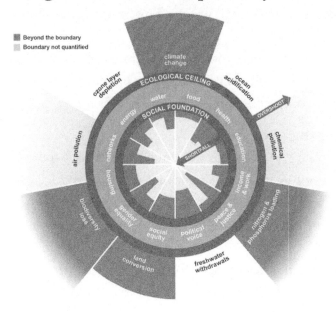

Image: Kate Raworth and Christian Guthier (2017)

Steady-state economies

We can flesh this economic doughnut model out a bit further with the idea of a steady-state economy. A steady-state economy has a constant stock of material wealth and a constant population size.

The notion of a steady-state economy, rather than a perpetual growth economy, has a distinguished lineage. Adam Smith, the father of modern economics, wrote his classic book *The Wealth of Nations* in 1776. Smith developed the idea of a stationary state of an economy. He believed that any national economy would eventually settle into a final steady-state.

In 1977 Herman Daly's seminal book *Steady-State Economics* brought the topic into modern times and gave birth to ecological economics. A flavour of this thinking is given by his saying, "Enough is best." If it is true that we need to move away from a growth economy towards a more steady-state one, this raises a central question: How can we move from the present economic system towards a more steady-state doughnut economic system? Here are some of the central changes that seem necessary.

Changing the tax system

We need some way to price the environment and the natural world into our economic systems. Economic systems produce goods, mainly products and services. They also produce 'bads', such as environmental damage and inequality. Traditionally we tax 'goods', but not 'bads'.

This is starting to change, for example with the introduction of carbon taxes, but they are not yet widespread, and they are at too low a level to be effective in stopping greenhouse warming. Only one fifth of global emissions are priced in this way and the average is \$3/ton. To be effective, all emissions would need to be priced at \$75/ton by 2030 to have a chance of limiting warming to 1.5-2°C.

As an aside, people often wonder what the difference is between carbon taxes and carbon credits. Briefly, a carbon tax is a tax on the burning of fossil fuels to incentivise the switch to green energy. Carbon credits are tradeable certificates that set a maximum level of emissions for companies, industries, or countries. Both have pros and cons and there is much controversy about them. In my opinion, global legislation to progressively reduce fossil fuel production would probably work better than either, but back now to taxation.

We would need to transition our present system away from taxing 'goods' with one which taxes all 'bads', not just CO_2 taxes. The main objection to this is that it would make everything too expensive. And it would if it were done on its own. In 2018, French President Emmanuel Macron had to drop his eco-tax on fuel in the face of massive resistance by the gilets jaunes (yellow vest) protesters for just this reason.

If all taxes were progressively shifted from 'goods' to 'bads', then income tax and VAT (sales taxes) could disappear. This would help but would not be enough. Hence the proposals for so-called cap and dividend. This is equivalent to a proposal for a carbon tax, with a significant amount of the proceeds paid equally to citizens as a dividend.

Cap and dividend systems solve the problem of carbon taxes bearing most heavily on the poor who spend a much higher proportion of their income on energy than do the wealthy. The dividend ensures that the poor are better off because of such carbon taxes.

We can imagine this principle spreading to a range of taxes covering all aspects of environmental damage. Redesigning this aspect of the economic system would go a long way to dealing with the problems of exceeding our planetary boundaries.

Changing economic growth

However, this does not tackle the serious problem of economic growth on a finite and vulnerable planet, nor does it directly deal with the problem of meeting our social needs. Let's look at the issue of economic growth first.

One of the primary causes of economic growth is the way our monetary system works. This is explored in *Modernising Money: Why Our Monetary System Is Broken and How It Can Be Fixed* by Andrew Jackson and Ben Dyson. As Martin Wolf, Chief Economic Commentator of the Financial Times said:

"The essence of the contemporary monetary system is the creation of money, out of nothing, by private banks' often foolish lending."

It is not widely known that 97% of money is brought into existence by the banks' ability to create loans out of thin air. Nor is it widely known that this is the primary cause of growth and the boom and bust economic cycles that create so much social damage. In optimistic upturns, banks create too many loans, and in pessimistic downturns, too few.

This not only leads to economic instability and financial crises. It has also produced the highest ever levels of personal and government debt, made houses unaffordable, and driven the short-termism which is destroying businesses and the ecosystems on which we all depend.

Bank loans directly stimulate growth by pumping money into the economy. If you borrow, you have to repay with interest. If you are a business, that interest can only be repaid by growth. Look no further than this for one of the primary causes of economic growth.

What is to be done? The book *Modernising Money* examines this in depth. It looks at how a UK law, implemented in 1844, could be updated and combined with reform proposals from the Great Depression to provide the UK with a stable monetary and banking system. This would result in much lower levels of personal debt, and a thriving economy with lower growth.

How? The core of Jackson and Dyson's proposal is to withdraw the right to create money from private banks and give it instead to a completely independent Money Creation Committee. This Money Creation Committee would only be able to create money if inflation were low and stable. This raises the question of how exactly this newly created money could be introduced into the economy.

Newly created money could be injected into the economy by one, or a combination, of four main methods:

- Government spending
- Cutting taxes
- Direct payments to citizens
- Paying down the national debt

Apart from the other benefits of this system, it would align well with the funding of many of the other proposals for change such as Doughnut Economics, a GND, and a Citizens' Income. It also addresses the main objection to all projects for social change: we can't afford it.

How can we afford it?

Exploring this a little further, I'd like to start with a quote from John Maynard Keynes, one of our greatest economists, and father of Keynesian economics which was the foundation of the post-war golden period of capitalism:

"Assuredly we can afford this and much more. Anything we can actually do, we can afford."

Another school of economics aligns well with the above approach and also deals with the 'but we can't afford it' objection. Known as Modern Monetary Theory, it is based on the idea that governments with their own sovereign currency, such as the pound in the UK, can, and should, create as much money as is needed to soak up any underused capacity in the economy. Once any unused capacity, such as unemployment, has been brought into use, any further printing of money will simply cause inflation to rise. This is the only real limit to the amount of money created.

Stephanie Kelton, a professor of economics in the USA, is one of the best-known proponents of this in her book, *The Deficit Myth: How to Build a Better Economy*. She clearly explains why a national economy is a completely different system to a household economy and so why a government with its own currency cannot go broke or become insolvent, as a household can.

She also explains why austerity or increasing taxes is not a necessity but a political choice, and why the national debt will not make our children poorer. For most of us, realising that austerity was a political choice made for ideological reasons and was a means of social engineering is a real eye-opener. All that needless suffering, and for what? So that the rich can become even richer?

Kelton challenges us to imagine a people's economy and gives us the tools to make it happen. Again, this kind of economic system will be needed if we are to invest in boosting the welfare state to deliver greater wellbeing for most people. And it will be needed to invest in the truly sustainable technologies capable of resolving climate change and our other environmental issues.

The Bank of England has created around £900 billion since 2008 in quantitative easing, effectively creating money, to prop up the failing economy. When we realise that the scale on which we need to mobilise to deal with the climate crisis is way beyond a war footing, then we can create the money to do it. As Keynes pointed out, the real limit is what we have the capability to do, not the finances for it.

Designing fair and just systems

Finally, in redesigning a financial system and determining levels of taxation and of financial equality, there is a profound thought experiment designed to clarify fair organising principles. It is called 'The Veil of Ignorance' and was made famous by the influential American moral philosopher, John Rawls. It applies as much to redesigning a political system as a financial one.

Imagine you are setting up an economic and political system, but you don't know your place in it. You don't know your class, social status, age, wealth, race, intelligence, or other abilities. What kind of a system would you design?

Rawls thought long and hard about the moral issues behind the design of our economic and political systems. A recent book (2023) by the London School of Economics philosopher and economist, Daniel Chandler, clarifies Rawls's thinking and maps it onto our present situation. It's called *Free and Equal – What Would a Fair Society Look Like?*

He takes Rawls's egalitarian and humane liberalism and carefully builds an irresistible case for a progressive agenda which would fundamentally reshape our society for the better. He shows how we can protect free speech and transcend the culture wars, get money out of politics, and create a more equal society where everyone has the chance to fulfil their potential while staying within the safe operating limits of this planet. I found it inspirational as a blueprint for a better future.

A new economic system

We're now about half way through this tour of economics, and the foundations are laid for putting together the kinds of change we need to see. Taking all these different ideas together, they give us the core of a new economic system that is fit for the dual purpose of increasing both personal and environmental wellbeing. Here's a summary of the main points.

Doughnut Economics gives us a target of the just and safe space that a new economic system must be designed to create. Steady-state economics provides a stable and truly sustainable equilibrium to aim at. Modernising money in line with Modern Monetary Theory creates a stable monetary system which can afford the changes we need. Changing the taxation system from taxing 'goods' to 'bads' is a fiscal policy that promotes good environmental practice. A range of taxes on excessive wealth and income directly promotes a more financially equal society; and this in turn directly promotes all the main aspects of social wellbeing.

Other promising new taxes that have been gaining support include a transaction tax on short term capital flows. It was originally proposed by another economist, James Tobin, to discourage short-termism in foreign currency exchange. A broader reaching version of this is the Robin Hood tax. This would affect a wide range of asset classes including the purchase and sale of bonds, commodities, mutual funds, unit trusts, and all financial derivatives. Together these taxes would limit the damage of the banking sector and raise huge funds for the new investments we need.

The role of the state

All these changes to the economic system point to a major re-balancing of the roles of the state and the market. To create the new systems that will work for us, the state has to take on a bigger and more proactive role, much as it did in World War II. It has to take on a mission to tackle effectively the 'wicked' problems we face. If you remember, a so-called wicked problem is one which is difficult or impossible to solve because of its exceedingly complex and interconnected nature.

One of the best explorations of this new role for government is by Mariana Mazzucato, Professor of Economics at the London School of Economics, in her most recent book, *Public Purpose* and *Mission Economy – a Moonshot Guide to Changing Capitalism*. To resolve our current wicked problems, we need the kind of new governance approach she outlines aiming our collective resources, at scale and speed, at the biggest problems we have ever faced. Only a transformed progressive state would have the capacity to carry out the kind of radical GND which we need.

Business world changes

However, we will also need changes at all levels, and in all parts of our economic operating systems. The biggest single part is the business sector, which is estimated to form around 70% of GDP. Small and medium sized businesses account for more than 90% of this. Collectively, business is probably the biggest organiser of human activity. It produces both the goods and services, and the 'bads', the carbon dioxide, the chemical pollution, the resource depletion, and much of the other damage to the natural world, as well as financial inequalities.

One of our biggest problems here, is how exactly to reduce the 'bads' whilst continuing to produce the 'goods'? First, the size of the problem can be reduced by a range of initiatives designed to do just that. One example is planned obsolescence. Many of the goods we buy are designed to last for far less time than they could be. Why? Because this is more profitable for the manufacturer.

We have the technical capability to produce goods that can last considerably longer, are more repairable, more recyclable and minimise environmental damage. Simple legislation can change this and reduce the scale of the harm. It has been estimated that planned obsolescence costs each of us around £50,000 over a lifetime. I couldn't find figures, but my guess is that if planned obsolescence were illegal, we would spend at least 10% less on the goods we buy.

A second example is advertising. In the USA, some 20% of GDP goes on advertising. Typically, it accounts for around 7-8% of the cost of what you buy. Imagine if advertising were illegal. In its place could be a publicly funded 'Which' consumer advice service. The probable effect would be to reduce the consumption of goods and services by some 10%. The two examples above would, I estimate, reduce material demand by around 20%. And there are other measures that we could take.

The role of business in creating a better world

However, if business is the main producer of the social and ecological damage caused by the unintended consequences of the present version of capitalism, what is to be done?

I'll start by mentioning the good outliers, the most progressive businesses. There are many and their numbers are growing rapidly. One of the earlier ones was Unilever with their Sustainable Living Plan started in 2011 under Paul Polman, who says:

"Most businesses operate and say how can I use society and the environment to be successful? We are saying the opposite – how can we contribute to the society and the environment to be successful?"

Over 10 years just a few of the goals Unilever achieved included:

- Reaching 1.3 billion people through their health and hygiene programs
- Reducing waste footprint per consumer by 32%
- Achieving zero waste in their factories
- Reducing greenhouse gas emissions in their manufacturing by 65%
- Achieving 100% renewable grid energy across their sites

Unilever did this and at the same time improved its position relative to the competition. Sustainable business works. There are many other examples of outstanding business practice out there. *The Business of Building a Better World* edited by David Cooperrider and Audrey Selian covers different examples from diverse businesses. And this trend is growing, but not fast enough.

One main reason is that to a significant extent, these progressive businesses are swimming against the current. At the moment, most businesses have a legal duty to maximise profit for the shareholders, regardless of consequences for society and the environment.

From 2010 a new form of incorporation was started as an alternative, the B Corporation, certified by the B Lab. Originally derived from the USA term 'benefit corporation', it includes measures of the positive impact on society and the environment, along with profit. This started a growth trend. Today there are more than 4,000 B Corps across 77 countries and 153 industries. You will probably know some of them: Ben and Jerry's, Patagonia.

They are a big improvement on the 'for profit' only corporation, but the glitch is in the 'profit' bit of B Corps. It may be that we need a different kind of corporation for a different kind of economy.

Imagine another kind of corporation, the W Corporation, the Wellbeing Corporation. The hypothetical Wellbeing Corporation would have only two legal responsibilities. To further wellbeing for people, and to further wellbeing for the planet.

Future Guardians

As I was writing this, another new book came out. *Building Tomorrow – Averting Economic Crisis with a New Economic System* by Paddy Le Flufy. He outlines a new economic system similar to the outline above, including Doughnut Economics, the circular economy and sovereign money. He also adds in a new business model, Future Guardians, which goes a step further than the B Corporation. It was developed by Riversimple, the UK's only small hydrogen car manufacturer, itself an inspiring story. Future Guardians is designed for use within the UK Limited Company legal framework and involves only rewriting the articles of association and Riversimple provide a template for this which Le Flufy spells out in Appendix B of his book.

The Future Guardians framework specifies six main stakeholders:

- The environment
- Customers
- Community
- Staff
- Investors
- Commercial partners

This goes considerably further than B Corporations. To make it comprehensive I, like Le Flufy, would add one more stakeholder:

- Humanity

With these seven main stakeholders built into the articles of association, and properly represented, we have an all-inclusive legal framework for future business and other forms of organisation. At the moment there are few Future Guardian companies but, if it were to be adopted by progressive companies such as Patagonia or Ben and Jerry's, the framework could well spread rapidly.

Le Flufy also includes in his six key components of a future economy two other elements which haven't been covered yet: regenerative organisations and complementary currencies. I summarise his work below.

Regenerative organisations

Regenerative organisations are ones which give back to our planet and our society more than they take. If we are to have a long term truly sustainable society, most of our organisations will need to be regenerative. Economically regenerative organisations use novel organisational structures and networks to foster ecosystems of community groups and local businesses. They support regeneration not extraction, localisation not centralisation, and resilience not reliance on brittle supply chains. We are at the early stages of this journey, but here are a few examples of different organisations which are pioneering the way.

Open Source Ecology

This is a visionary organisation. They are creating a group of "the 50 most important machines that it takes for modern life to exist". These include things such as a tractor, an oven, and a circuit maker. They are designed so they can be used in combinations to create any machine required.

This set of 50 machines are called the Global Village Construction Set and should provide all that is needed to build, or rebuild, the infrastructures of modern civilisation. By going open source, they are providing a new economic model for distributive enterprise. Every community in the world could produce everything they need. This could be a critical resource in the face of civilisation collapse.

Bendigo Community Banks

These were started in Australia in the 1990s to revitalise their local communities as well as to provide local banking services when local banks closed down. The model is both regenerative and financially viable, and there are over 300 branches. The communities invest in setting up their branches and Bendigo provides capital and banking services. Much of their profit is distributed in the local community.

Fab Labs

Short for Fabrication Laboratories, these were started by MIT in the USA based on research on how to turn data into things and things into data. They have state-of-the-art facilities to analyse and manipulate materials to make almost anything. There was massive popular demand and Fab Labs spread worldwide as an open-source regenerative organisation. Manufacturing data for any design is uploaded to Fab Cloud and is available for anyone to make.

Transition Network

This began in Totnes, England in 2006 and was started by Rob Hopkins. It spread to become a network of local initiatives who support projects to help their local communities to become more sustainable, to combat climate change, and to address social inequality. Today Transition is a global network of thousands of groups in 50 countries. A recent initiative, Bounce Forward, has become Transition Together and aims to rebuild our shared imagination and envisioning a better future for 2030.

These are just four examples and they each have different organisational structures designed to achieve their differing visions and purposes. If you are in a more traditional business, a book worth checking out is Frederic Laloux's *Re-Inventing Organisations: A Guide to Creating Organisations Inspired by the Next Stage in Human Consciousness.*

Complementary currencies

An important aspect of any economy is the currency it uses. There is an old saying, "If the only tool you have is a hammer, you will start treating all your problems like a nail". We take it for granted that there is only one kind of money, the one we are used to. This isn't true. Even traditional money comes in two different kinds. Every country either has a sovereign currency, issued by the state, or it adopts the currency of another country, usually the dollar. The UK has a sovereign currency. If we had joined the Euro, we would not have a sovereign currency and this would make us very vulnerable to the ups and downs of the Euro, as Greece discovered to its cost.

Apart from the traditional national currency, there are many other forms of currency. They work in different ways and have different strengths and weaknesses. Complementary currencies are designed to complement traditional currencies, not to replace them, hence the name. There are compelling arguments for using a variety of currencies rather than just one. One of the strongest is that if instead of a currency monoculture we had an ecosystem of different currencies, then our economic system would be more resilient in the face of international financial fluctuations.

The late Bernard Lietaer once said, "Give me a social or environmental problem, and I will design a currency to solve it". His book, *Rethinking Money: How New Currencies Turn Scarcity Into Prosperity* written with Jacqui Dunne, is one of the best expositions of why the current monetary system needs changing and the role that complementary currencies can play in this.

Local currencies

Local currencies have been designed and used with widely varying purposes. They can help money to stay local, improving local prosperity by reducing the export of money from the area by big business. There are many examples of this in different countries and they usually have a 1:1 exchange rate with the local currency. The Brixton Pound is an example in the UK which has since morphed into a digital local currency.

Poverty reduction currencies

Complementary currencies can be designed to reduce poverty. Banco Parmas, set up in a poor Brazilian town in the late 1990s, was a local currency which did just this. The currency was estimated to have tripled the effect of development aid, created over 1,800 jobs, and triggered the development of similar currencies across Brazil. This is an important contribution to the challenging job or reducing financial inequality.

Currencies to incentivise

Currencies can be used to create incentives to do useful things which wouldn't otherwise get done by traditional money. Curitiba Bus Tokens, also in Brazil, was designed to incentivise one type of activity by mediating a single type of exchange.

Curitiba had extensive slums with a big rubbish problem and unaffordable bus fares. Skips were placed on the edge of the slums to collect three kinds of rubbish: recyclable, bio-waste, and landfill. Anyone could collect and sort rubbish from the slums and were repaid in bus tokens. Simple and effective.

Currencies to combat recessions and depressions

Complementary currencies were used to great effect to combat the Great Depression back in the 1930s. The Worgl was created in the town of Worgl in Austria as a currency that depreciated in value by 1% each month. This had the effect of encouraging spending, since if you didn't use the currency it lost value. It was successful, the local economy grew, and many other towns copied it. Unfortunately, the Austrian Central Bank got worried that it was too successful and the government banned it! To this day there exist many business-to-business complementary currencies.

Local Exchange Trading Systems

Another kind of currency is designed to increase the range of economic activity for those who are cash poor and use a currency based on time, the hours of work done. The Local Exchange Trading System, LETS, is an example of this.

A local LETSystem has an agreed local currency usually based on an hour of work and all work is usually done at the same rate per hour.

You can usually trade goods too. When you 'buy' something, your account goes into debit, and when you 'sell' it is credited.

In the UK there is a national networking organisation called Letslink UK Network.

Time Banking

There are many other banking systems with a variety of purposes. The Volunteer Labour Bank in Osaka, Japan, started in 1973, is the world's first known time bank. It spread to the USA in the eighties, making it the first international time banking organisation. It enables people with distant aging relatives to care for someone locally in exchange for their loved one being looked after elsewhere. It also allows exchanges across time; you can contribute care now and draw it out later when you need it. The system has evolved into a variety of forms in Japan and plays a major role in caring for the elderly.

Complementary currencies have huge potential to evolve into a complex ecosystem of currencies which can add resilience and diversity to our economic systems.

Summary so far

We have looked at some key changes which will be needed if we are to create an economy which is able to serve our human needs and those of the living Earth. Doughnut Economics provides an economic target of a just and sustainable space in which humanity can flourish.

Modern Monetary Theory provides the economic framework for modernising money and creating the basis for more of a steady-state economy which frees us from the dire threats of exponentially increasing economic growth. It can also, in combination with the other changes outlined, enable us to make the massive investments needed to green our infrastructures, for example by way of GNDs, so they become truly sustainable.

The tax system can be redesigned to be more fair and just, in part by taxing 'bads' instead of 'goods', but also by being more redistributive. The state will need to become more innovative as the only body with the capability to bring about all the above changes.

And the business world, making up 70% of the global economy, will have a central role to play in effecting the necessary transformations to create an economy which serves the needs of people and the planet.

Looking at the part the business world would need to play, good intentions are not enough. You can only manage what you can measure. Our predominant measure is money, or more specifically profit. It's fine to legislate for business representing the interest of a wide range of stakeholders, as B Corporations or Future Guardian legal forms do, and as the hypothetical Wellbeing Corporation could. But we will need new and different metrics, or measures, other than profit alone by which to manage the ecologically sound businesses which we need now and for the future. What might these new metrics be? They will need to focus on measuring environmental damage and human wellbeing.

Different measures for business

I'll mention first just two major insights into how this may be achieved. They come from the work of Per Espen Stoknes, the Director of the Centre for Sustainability and Energy at the Norwegian Business School in Oslo. His book, *Tomorrow's Economy: A Guide to Creating Healthy Green Growth* outlines these, and much more. These two insights are both measures of productivity and, if you can measure something, you can manage it.

The first is a measure of carbon productivity. This is the idea that we need to decrease the amount of carbon dioxide we produce each year for each unit of business productivity. For example, to achieve the goal of limiting warming to 2°C by 2050, we will need to improve our carbon productivity by 6-7% on average every year until then, starting slowly, then increasing each year.

The figure will be much higher if we want to stay within 1.5°C of warming. Some estimates say that greenhouse gas emissions must peak before 2025 and decline by 43% before 2030.

Stoknes introduces the term CAPRO to stand for carbon productivity, which he defined as the value added per ton of carbon dioxide per year, £/tCO_2pa. He also uses 'capro' to stand for the rate of change in CAPRO in percent per year. If this measure were a legal requirement in corporate accounting, with stiff tax penalties for not meeting it, this would transform how businesses function. They would have to reduce their carbon every year, and this is just what's needed.

Of course, 'capro' only accounts for one aspect of business pollution. But it would set an important precedent and could lead to productivity improvements in all other measures of both pollution and resource depletion. Next would be the two other main greenhouse gases, methane and nitrous oxides, which may be called 'mepro' and 'nipro'. Then there are all the other pollutants. These could be ranked in order of damage to humans and our ecosystems; 'nepros' for neonicotinoids, and so on.

Per Espen Stoknes's second innovation is the concept of social productivity, SOPRO, as an annual measure of fair and inclusive growth, with 'sopro' being the % change annually. While resource productivity is defined as the ratio of value creation to resource use, social productivity would be the ratio of value creation to financial inequality.

Just as measuring carbon productivity can be used to reduce carbon emissions, so measuring social productivity can be used to reduce social inequality as measured by financial inequality. Why financial inequality?

Remember, from the earlier mention of *The Spirit Level: Why Equality is Better for Everyone*, most social ills increase in direct proportion to financial inequality, while overall social wellbeing increases with financial equality. So, measuring financial inequality gives a good estimate of general social wellbeing; less inequality means more wellbeing.

Measuring financial inequality

This raises the important question of how best to measure social inequality. The first main measure was the Gini coefficient, or the Gini index, developed by the Italian statistician, Corrado Gini. It is based on the difference between the observed income distribution and a perfectly equal income distribution.

A perfectly equal income distribution would give a score of 0.0, and a perfectly unequal distribution, in which one person owns everything, would be 1.0. In general terms, a Gini index of under 0.2 is reasonably close to perfect income distribution. 0.2-0.3 corresponds with relative equality. 0.3-0.4 corresponds with significant level of inequality. 0.4-0.5 signifies a high-income disparity. And 0.5 or above means extreme inequality. The Gini index is often expressed as a percentage, so 0.5 becomes 50%.

Here are a few figures from the World Bank on the ranking of 162 different countries on financial inequality:

- South Africa, no 1 at 63%

- USA 46th at 41.5%
- UK 93rd at 35.1%
- Finland 148th at 27.7%
- The Slovak Republic is the most equal at 23.2%

In practice a new index, the Palma ratio, is rapidly replacing the Gini Index because it works better. The Palma ratio is the share of income taken by the top 10% of earners divided by the share of income taken by the bottom 40% of earners. The higher the Palma score, the greater the inequality. As with the Gini, lower is better.

It's based on the work of Gabriel Palma, a Chilean economist, who found that middle class incomes usually account for half the national income, while the other half is split between the top 10% and the bottom 40%. If we're interested in inequality, then almost all the action takes place between the latter two groups. The Palma ratio is much more sensitive to these groups, whilst the Gini index is more sensitive to the middle range. This is why more bodies, such as the UN, are adopting the Palma ratio.

Here are the figures for the Palma ratio:

- Worst is South Africa at 6.89
- USA 1.79
- UK 1.49
- Finland 0.89
- Best is Slovakia at 0.81

The Palma ratio would be a good measure to use for SOPRO, and the annual % change, 'sopro'. As with 'capro', we can imagine this could be diversified into a range of other areas of social wellbeing. Perhaps racial integration as 'rapro', gender equality as 'gepro', and so on. The main point is that we have good ways of measuring and changing social equality, and these can be built into our economic systems.

Evolving forms of business organisation

Together, these new measures, or metrics, would transform the goals and functioning of our hypothetical Wellbeing Corporation of the future. This is not just wishful thinking. Perhaps the closest thing to the Wellbeing Corporation at the moment is the cooperative movement.

Not many people realise how big the cooperative movement is. One estimate indicates that almost 10% of the world's population work in over 3 million cooperatives and mutuals; and they are growing rapidly. The Mondragon Cooperative of Spain is the biggest, and perhaps the best known. Alongside the cooperatives themselves we have their close relatives: mutuals, social enterprises, employee-owned companies, community land trusts, and more.

To summarise, there are three main types of corporation. The vast majority of the world's businesses are for profit corporations. The cooperatives are widespread but variable in their representation of all the different stakeholders. By comparison, the B Corps movement is as yet very small, but growing fast. And the possible Wellbeing Corporation does not exist yet, although Future Guardians, with humanity as an additional stakeholder, is the closest thing to it.

There is a strong argument for using legislation to phase 'profit only' companies down and out, whilst cooperatives, B Corps, and then Wellbeing Corporations are phased in sequentially. This could, for example, be done by bringing in a legal requirement for CAPRO and SOPRO accounting, with an annual requirement for increasing the productivity of each.

Evolving the functioning of economic systems

Together with a gradual change in taxation from 'goods' to 'bads', all the economic changes outlined can give us a way of rapidly evolving our economic systems, enabling them to produce more of what we want them to, which as you well know by now, is wellbeing for ourselves and for the natural world.

As these new economic forms grow, the effect will be to rapidly shut down all the main unintended consequences of the neoliberal version of capitalism. The economic system would move from being exploitative to being regenerative. As inequality decreases, social equality increases. As carbon dioxide emissions decrease, and other pollutants too, our ecosystems can begin their slow recovery.

Changing the purpose of the economic system

There is a common thread that runs through these explorations of different possibilities for our economic systems. This thread unites the ideas about changing our monetary system to provide a stable economy that can finance the massive changes we need to make. It unites the changes we can make in the fiscal systems to tax 'bads' rather than 'goods'. And it unites the changes to the corporate structures that rule the world of business.

The common thread is this: to change the goals of the systems in question. In systems thinking, this is one of the most powerful interventions you can make to change what a system actually does. And remember again, a system is what a system does.

The timescale of transition to a transformed economy

As well as a common thread, there is also a common subtext. All the changes mapped out above on how to transform our economic systems, and outlined in the next section on the British GND, will take time. Some changes will be relatively fast: for example, changing the taxation system and accompanying legislation could well be done within a year.

At the other end of the spectrum are the slow and capital-rich investments we will need to make in, for example, our energy infrastructures as we change them over from fossil fuel reliance to sustainable energy sources. Ten years is probably a feasible timescale for this, given the scale of the emergency.

If this is so, I believe we will need some kind of ten-year transition plan to make sense of this massive and potentially chaotic process. This will allow organisations of all kinds to see the direction and speed of travel, and to make plans accordingly. The GND which we looked at briefly, gives a framework for the emerging new journey. It also fleshes out the new economic thinking we've just been looking at. All of this gives us hope for the future. We know what we have to do to create the kind of economic systems we need. And so, at last, we come to the end of this critically important chapter.

And, by the way, well done for hanging in there as we explored the murky depths of economic systems! Economics is not called the dismal science for nothing. Actually, when looking at neoliberal economics, it is more an ideology than a science. And, being based on so-called 'Homo Economicus', a short sighted and self-centred version of humankind, the term dismal ideology seems to fit well.

On next to the sunnier uplands of the Green New Deal.

Chapter Seven
The Green New Deal and Earth for All

The GND that we looked at earlier was based on the American version of the GND. The British version is shaping up to be different in a few main respects. It leans more heavily on the notion of the entrepreneurial state as the major driving force. And it is more international in its focus and application.

As I've said before, there is a wide range of GNDs, from GND-lite, based on neoliberal economics, to GND-radical, which gets to the heart of the systemic causes of our shared ills. There are many books which between them cover the spectrum of GNDs; on my bookshelves there are six different GND books. I'll draw most heavily on *The Case for the Green New Deal* by Ann Pettifor, a British economist who advises governments and organisations and predicted the Great Financial Crisis of 2008. This British GND (BGND), in my opinion, best addresses the underlying systemic causes of our problems.

The origins of the GND were in the UK. A report was released by the GND Group, of which Colin Hines was the convenor and Ann Pettifor, Caroline Lucas, Tony Juniper, and Jeremy Leggett were founder members. It was published by the New Economics Foundation in 2008 and outlined a series of policy proposals to tackle global warming, the financial crisis and peak oil. They mapped out seven main principles.

Principle One: A Steady-state Economy

A steady-state economy is designed not to exceed the nine main planetary boundaries. To recap: climate change, biodiversity loss, chemical pollution and novel entities, ocean acidification, freshwater consumption, land-system change, nitrogen and phosphorus flows, and aerosols in the atmosphere.

A steady-state economy would minimise waste with closed loop recycling methods for materials and waste. It would be based on the development of circular resource and energy networks in the places where people live and work. The aim is to keep the stock of physical capital and material goods steady, while economic social activity rebuilds overall system health.

Known as the circular economy, the three core principles are: eliminate waste and pollution, circulate products and materials, and regenerate nature. This is a profoundly different basis for an economy when compared to our present linear 'take, make, use and waste' model. The circular economy is well explored in *The Circular Economy: A Wealth of Flows* by Ken Webster of the Ellen MacArthur Foundation.

Principle Two: Limited Needs, Not Limitless Wants

As Mahatma Gandhi famously put it three-quarters of a century ago: *"The world has enough for everyone's needs, but not everyone's greed."*

The BGND approach to the breakdown of Earth's systems is to reverse the dominant paradigm of neoliberal capitalism. A paradigm is a worldview, or set of core beliefs underpinning a particular subject, in this case orthodox economics. Paradigms have their power through being a set of largely unconsciously held shared beliefs.

What is emerging is a 'paradigm shift' in our thinking. The term paradigm shift comes from the physicist and philosopher Thomas

Kuhn in his influential book back in the sixties, *The Structure of Scientific Revolutions*.

What is to replace the old paradigm? Perhaps the simplest, and most comprehensive, model is Kate Raworth's economic doughnut with its safe operating space for humanity. This model is underpinned by a set of core beliefs which run through the entire BGND proposals and indeed, through much else of what you have been reading here.

Is the purpose of the economy to meet human wants or human needs? Our current system places the emphasis on increasing the standard of living through attempting to satisfy our apparently limitless human material wants. In contrast, the emerging new economy places the emphasis on improving the quality of life through better meeting our basic human needs and those of nature.

I think there's an important question here for each of us as we navigate life's complexities. Do you prefer to live in a society which offers an increasing material standard of living at the cost of a decreasing quality of life, but ultimately collapses? Or would you rather live in a society which offers an increasing quality of life at the cost of a decreasing material standard of living, but is sustainable in the long-term? In short, would you rather be richer and more miserable, or poorer but happier? Quality of life or quantity of stuff. Something to ponder... and that's aside from that question of collapse.

Principle Three: Self-Sufficiency

The UK oil and gas industries are effectively subsidised to the tune of some £13 billion annually. Globally the figure is around £6,000 billion annually, some 7% of global GDP. By contrast, sustainable energy is only subsidised globally by around £140 billion, some 0.16% of global GDP. This ridiculous situation is systemic madness and has to change.

And when it does change, we will no longer be shipping stuff around the world as though there were no tomorrow. We will have to become more locally self-sufficient at every level from the national to the neighbourhood area. One consequence is the countries of the Global South will become freer to throw off the shackles of modern economic colonialism and become more autonomous, having the freedom to manage their own affairs with their economic policy making.

All nations will become more autonomous in meeting the needs of their citizens in terms of goods and services. All other areas, such as ideas, innovations, and art will remain international. More will be produced locally. At the household level, sufficiency will become more predominant, but at the public level shared wealth will be more widely available.

George Monbiot put the case for this well in a Guardian article some five years ago, entitled: "Public luxury for all or private luxury for some; this is the choice we face." His summary of what works best is private sufficiency and public luxury.

Imagine our country having not just free and outstanding quality health and education services, but also free public transport, more parks, trees, green areas and allotments, flourishing cultural activities, more electric car-pooling, co-housing developments, and so on. You get the idea.

Principle Four: A Mixed-Market Economy

Extraordinary levels of collective effort will be required to move our society away from the extractive and fossil-fuel based economy of the past towards the green and truly sustainable economy of the future. The scale of activity required will be well beyond the scale of effort put into World War II.

We've already looked at the role of the re-invigorated state in bringing about a transformative GND. It will need regulatory and taxation powers to bring about the changes in all sectors and at all levels of the economy. With approaches like Stafford Beer's viable systems, it will be participatory, de-centralising and anti-bureaucratic; it will be an entrepreneurial and human-centred state. Our views of this transformed state will be very different from our views of the current state. They will be more like those in Finland where they think well of their state.

However, the transformation of the economy needs more than the efforts of the state. It needs a vibrant and flourishing market economy to complement, support, and gain from the activities of the state. Market economies have flourished and served us well over more than 5,000 years, and they will flourish again in this new green economy.

The state will invest in the big transformational projects: the transition to the new infrastructures for a sustainable economy, the improved public transport, the retrofitting of our housing stock to much higher levels of insulation, and so forth. All this is affordable with a new economic system. The bulk of the work will be done by local labour in the local area by small businesses that function more like cooperatives or Wellbeing Corporations. It will be well-paid work generating income and wealth, and more of which will stay in our local communities.

Principle Five: A Labour Intensive Economy

As implied above, the emerging new economy will be more labour intensive. Fossil fuels will be replaced by a combination of the new sustainable energy sources: solar energy, wind turbines, green hydrogen, geothermal energy, and so on. But we will need more human labour, for example, to improve our growing range of welfare services, such as care services, and to provide extensive retraining for the workforce. We will also need people power for the more sustainable forms of agriculture: agroforestry, mixed farming, permaculture, multiple cropping, and so forth. And we will need more people to accelerate tree planting and rewilding to draw down carbon and replenish the biodiversity of the natural world.

Hence the American GND's promise of a 'job guarantee', and the British GND's promise of a 'carbon army'. Both public and private sectors will create a growing range of highly skilled jobs, with meaningful work providing decent wages.

The economy will be geared to creating purposeful work by the provision of universal basic services in health, education, housing, care, and so on. This is necessary to rebalance the economy towards meeting the human needs of all people, and away from the massive inequalities of late-stage neoliberal capitalism.

The idea of a Universal Basic Income (UBI) has become more popular as a way of addressing growing inequality. It may become a part of our future economy. But personally, I have several concerns about this. First, UBI is a sticking plaster treating the symptom rather than addressing the fundamental cause. This is not usually the winning strategy.

Second, UBI is both expensive and regressive. It is expensive because it would cost more than double the Department of Work and Pensions current budget. And it is regressive, benefiting the affluent more, because it is paid to all citizens regardless of their income or need, whilst not being enough to meet all needs of the poorest. The UBI is an expenditure equivalent to a flat tax rate.

The GND proposal to develop Universal Basic Services (UBS), rather than UBI, addresses the fundamental cause rather than the symptoms. By creating more decently paid jobs, and close to full employment, it massively reduces inequality. It addresses causes rather than symptoms, and pre-distributes income rather than redistributes it, as taxation does. However, there will still be some whom UBS does not reach. What of them?

A badly needed redesign of the benefits system can address this. Especially if it has as a backstop 'negative' income tax for those who fall through any holes in the welfare net. What is negative income tax? In the absence of any other income, all citizens whose income is below the minimum needed to survive adequately would have their income made up to that necessary minimum by the tax collection service, His Majesty's Revenue and Customs. This would provide a real and meaningful safety net for the poor, and would work much better than the current benefits system does.

Most importantly for the GND, universal services would provide the means to build meaningful work, cooperation, and solidarity – unity among individuals with a common interest. This will be much needed in a world where Earth systems are failing.

Principle Six: Monetary and Fiscal Coordination

Under the BGND, our monetary and fiscal institutions and policies will work together to support society as a whole, rather than to serve the interests of the few in the financial sector. We looked at how this may work in the chapter on economic systems. However, as this is so central to the BGND, and as economics mystifies most people, I will recap briefly.

We covered previously how the post-war golden age of social democratic capitalism was based on Keynesian economics. John Maynard Keynes developed what is now generally known as macroeconomics, the study of whole economies. Up until then, and for many neoliberal economists now, economics was the study of microeconomics, the study of the economics of individuals, households, and firms.

The relationship of macroeconomics to microeconomics is similar to the relationship of woods to trees. If you only study microeconomics, you can't see the wood for the trees. These are two different levels of the economic system, and they behave quite differently. This is why, as we've seen, the economy of a country is so different to that of a household; and why a country like the UK, with its own currency, can afford to repay any debt we incur. This is fundamental to financing the BGND and it deals with that constant refrain of politicians and the mass media: "But we can't afford it." We can.

Keynes focussed on the macroeconomy because, in the aftermath of the Great Depression, he was concerned with creating full employment. Full employment is fundamental to the BGND.

To create the full employment of the BGND, the main monetary authority, The Bank of England, supplies the 'macro' clients, government, banks, and pension funds, with loans and deposits.

It does this in the same way as commercial banks currently provide loans and deposits to 'micro' clients, firms and individuals.

To reiterate the key point here, when the government borrows in order to invest, it adds to the national debt. But the debt of a nation to its own citizens is a very different thing to the debt of a private individual or firm. It's a macroeconomic issue, not a microeconomic one. The nation is the sum of all its citizens, so to owe money to them is the equivalent of you owing money to yourself. It's a problem of perception; it's not a real problem.

The BGND economy will not be debt-free. However, its credit creation systems will be balanced by the tax revenues from near full employment. These will be used to repay loans and prevent the build-up of debt and deficits. This is the virtuous circle that leads to a steady-state financial system.

The monetary authorities will ensure that the value of the currency remains stable by managing the rate of interest. The fiscal authorities will spend and support investment in the productive activities needed to transform the economy. Again, this transformation is away from our present fossil-fuel based and material-growth focussed economy, and towards what we will need to thrive in future. That is, the goods and services which meet people's real needs and the needs of our ecosystems for recovery. As I've said, employment generates the taxes to repay the borrowing. It will be a good thing when politicians understand that the best way to increase tax revenues is not by raising taxes, but by expanding skilled and well-paid employment!

However, there is one important area that BGND proposals don't cover, a fly in the ointment that still bugs me. The wealthiest 10% of the world's population creates 50% of carbon dioxide pollution. The poorest 50% contributes only 10%. Cutting the carbon emissions of the wealthy would reduce global consumption by nearly 50% at a stroke. This would be a quick win in our struggle to reduce greenhouse gas emissions, but how could it be achieved?

Carbon taxes you might think. But a general carbon tax is highly regressive and would bear proportionately more heavily on the poor who, you will recall, pay a greater proportion of their income on energy intensive heating and transportation. I believe that some form of carbon taxation has a part to play, and perhaps one that includes citizens' dividends aimed primarily at the less well off. But it doesn't address the problem of high emissions by the wealthiest.

Perhaps a different approach altogether is needed. In the Second World War, when food was scarce, it was simply rationed. Should we introduce carbon rationing for the top 10%? We might ration their carbon emissions to the average national or European level.

This could be done by requiring them to submit their full carbon emissions as part of their tax returns. False returns and high emissions would be subject to penalties. What would it take to do the job? A stiff fine of a significant part of any income above the national average? A jail sentence? Another decision for a citizens' assembly I suspect.

Principle Seven: Abandon Delusions of Infinite Expansion

Previously we've looked at the idea of infinite growth on a finite planet, clearly a non-starter. The only people who seem to believe in it are our neoliberal economists. Unfortunately, they are the people who dominate our politicians' thinking. And that's why we constantly hear both politicians and the media telling us that we need more growth and a higher GDP. This paradigm has not shifted yet.

We've also looked at why GDP is not the best way to measure our economy. Before the Second World War, economists seldom talked of growth. Instead they discussed levels of economic activity. Was the level of employment, investment, or output too high or too low? What policy adjustments were needed? The idea of growth as the goal of the economy only became paramount in the fifties.

It was unwise neoliberal advice that led to the high inflation of the seventies, peaking at 23% in 1975. At the time, the right-wing media put all the blame on Keynesian economics, the Labour Party, and the unions. So ended the golden age of social democratic capitalism. If the truth were known, but for the vested interests we could have bypassed the last 40 years of neoliberalism and most of its problems.

There are many other measures of the economy which would work better than GDP. Perhaps the longest used one is the Gross National Happiness index (GNH) adopted by Bhutan in the early seventies. It is based on nine domains: psychological wellbeing, health, education, time use, cultural diversity and resilience, good governance, communal vitality, ecological diversity and resilience, and living standards.

I quite like the GNH because it targets the wellbeing of people and ecosystems more than most. But there are many others in use, all with their pros and cons. They include:

- Genuine Progress Indicator (GPI)
- Index of Human Development (HDI)
- Human Poverty Index (HPI)
- Index of Sustainable Economic Welfare (ISEW)
- Happy Planet Index (HPI)
- Green Gross Domestic Product (GGDP)

Any of these would work better than GDP. Time will tell which one wins. It may be that a bigger problem is that these are all single measures. A better idea, perhaps, is a dashboard of different measures, each of which targets different key areas. As I've suggested we could adopt the multiple dimensions of Kate Raworth's economic doughnut. This also aligns with the viable system model thinking outlined earlier.

Staying with the theme of growth for the moment, one argument that we can get caught up in is the growth vs de-growth one. Most say that lack of growth is bad.

Japan's lack of GDP growth shows otherwise. Whilst having no significant growth, Japan has experienced intact communities, low crime, almost non-existent drug use, world-class quality of food and consumer goods, with health and life expectancy being among the highest in the world.

One minor problem with the de-growth case is that it has the word growth built into it. Better perhaps to argue for a move towards a steady-state economy. Also, a critically important question that you seldom hear asked is, growth in what? It's not that growth itself is good or bad, but rather that growth in some things is bad: carbon dioxide emissions, pollution, material goods consumption and planetary resource depletion. Growth in other things is good: psychological wellbeing, education, health, good governance, and so forth. Perhaps the best policy is to be agnostic on the issue of growth as a whole.

One of the questions for environmental macroeconomics is that of optimal scale. How big would an optimal economy be? There are few estimates of this, and I'm not convinced it is one of the more important questions to focus on. Of greater significance is how much the richer countries contribute to global transformation. It seems clear to me that the richest countries have a moral obligation to make the biggest cuts in emissions, pollution, and environmental resource use. And to make the biggest financial contributions to the Global South in the rapid global transition to a truly sustainable world.

To summarise, the GND in general gives us one of our best and most popular economically viable frameworks for moving from the present uneconomic and damaging economy to a steady-state economy with an improving quality of life. I believe the GND will rise rapidly up the political agenda. But it is not the only contender out there, there are others.

Earth for All

Published in 2022, *Earth for All: A Survival Guide for Humanity* with multiple authors having considerable expertise, also has a website launched at the same time. Although recent, I think it looks promising. But first a little background.

Let's go back in time 50 years to 1972, the early years of environmental awareness. The UN had convened the first Earth Summit on the Human Environment in Stockholm. Just before this a small group of pioneering researchers at MIT published their remarkable book *The Limits to Growth* with Donella Meadows as the lead author, as I mentioned in the Introduction.

It was remarkable in a number of ways. First, it was based on the then new computer modelling of dynamic systems. The team at MIT sought to capture the complex dynamics of our human systems evolving on a finite planet. They did this by running different scenarios with different assumptions about growth rates in population, economics, resource usage, pollution, and so on. When they ran the 'business-as-usual' scenario, human society hit the buffers towards the end of the first half of the twenty-first century. This led, in their model, to a global collapse of the human population.

Here is the second remarkable aspect of the project. Its modelling of business-as-usual, the path we have been following, projected accurately the period of collapse we are now entering. To successfully predict a future event 50 years in advance is simply astonishing. It tells us that this technology of dynamic computer simulation can have a very high level of credibility. We will come back to why this is important.

The third remarkable aspect was the vehemence with which the project was attacked by the vested interests in the form of the media and politicians. Ronald Regan's quote earlier to the effect that there are no limits to growth goes to the heart of the matter. Orthodox economics and the capitalist system are based on unlimited growth; the core of their ideology was at stake.

Next, the important practical applications of all this. The dynamic computer simulations started at MIT have proliferated and become much more precise and useful. The current models have been exploring the most viable and effective interventions which we can still make. The models show how these interventions can work with a very high level of reliability.

However, we have a limited time window of around ten years, and this is another compelling argument for a ten-year transition plan. After that it is too late; we will have hit too many of the bad social and environmental tipping points.

Earth for All summarises this approach, and the key interventions which are necessary and sufficient to achieve the changes we need. Although it has evolved in a quite different way to the GND approach, the results of both are in surprisingly good alignment. Here are the five most effective key interventions:

- An end to poverty in one generation
- Greater equality among people and nations
- Food for healthy people on a healthy planet
- Truly sustainable energy for all
- A major upgrade of our economic system

The Earth for All campaign identifies fourteen main policy recommendations to achieve these goals. These are important both because they have tested on dynamic simulations and because they go some way to addressing the fundamental systemic problems.

On Poverty

- The International Monetary Fund (IMF) to allocate at least $1trillion annually to low-income countries for green jobs by creating investments through Special Drawing Rights.
- Cancel all debts to low-income countries with an average of less than $10,000 income per person.
- Protect fledgling industries in low-income countries. Promote trade between these countries. Improve access to renewables and health technologies by enabling technology transfer and removing intellectual property constraints.

On Inequality

- Increase taxes on the 10% richest until they take less than 40% of the national income. Close international loopholes for tax evasion by corporations and individuals, like transfer pricing and tax havens. Introduce strong progressive taxation on luxury carbon and biosphere consumption.
- Legislate to strengthen workers' rights.
- Introduce citizens' funds to provide all citizens with their fair share of income, wealth, and the global commons. Use carbon fee and dividend schemes to do this.
- Provide access to education for all girls and women.
- Achieve gender equality in both jobs and leadership roles.

As an aside, to these I would add policies to address the rights, and improve the conditions, of all minority groups: racial, religious, disability, and so on.

On Food

- Legislate to reduce food waste and loss.

- Increase economic incentives for all regenerative agriculture and sustainable intensification.
- Promote healthy diets within the planetary boundaries.

On Energy
- Phase out fossil fuels and scale up renewable and energy efficiency, including insulation, rapidly. Triple investments in renewables to over $1trillion annually in new renewables.
- Electrify everything.
- Invest in energy storage at scale.

I think these Earth for All proposals align well with those of the GND. We could imagine both sets of proposals being merged into a combined set.

All very well, but how do implement these changes?

For all the strengths of the Earth for All proposals, I think it has one main weakness, which is shared by the GND proposals. They both have little to say about *how* we change the political system to create the changes they propose.

If the economic system is the main cause of our problems, it can only be changed by the political system. The present political system demonstrates its continued inability to change the economic system and we've looked in depth at why this happens.

And so back to the Mandate

This is why I've spent so much time looking at how to make changes in the political system. And this is why I'm proposing the Citizens' Mandate for Change as the single most effective intervention to achieve this. If it grows exponentially, it is likely to give birth to a Citizens' Movement for Change, which has the potential through becoming a 'movement of movements', to be the biggest of all the movements for change. And, again, all this depends on you, what you think of it, and what you do. More on this next.

Talking about change

Taken together, the proposals and policies of the GND and Earth for All seem to me to be both plausible and credible. However, they also need to be compelling, and they can only be compelling if they are widely discussed. And that is where the conversations you have with friends, family, colleagues, and neighbours could turn out to be so much more important than is immediately obvious. We need to first imagine the future we want before we can bring it into being.

I've been encouraged by a couple of ideas and practices which have emerged during conversations with friends. One is the spontaneous emergence of discussion groups which meet face-to-face, or online, to explore and make sense of this thinking. Another is an interest in starting study groups, for the same purpose. Indeed, one of my reasons for taking the time to write about all this is to support such conversations for change. I've tried to distil some of the best thinking into simple ideas and plain English.

Since few of us have experience of major social transformation, we tend to underestimate the power of 'an idea whose time has come' phenomenon. Such ideas become infectious. As you consider all of this, another important thing to bear in mind is the alternative, business-as-usual. And business-as-usual means we are doomed.

On the positive side, discussions about the kind of transformations we're looking at will ripple out, and, I believe, will have a positive effect in many ways, including our shared level of hopefulness about the future. They will make it possible to redesign the many aspects of society that have become increasingly dysfunctional over the last four decades. At best, hard though it is to believe from where we are, we can begin to imagine a new golden age. So, where to go next?

Back again briefly to the Citizens' Mandate. If it is the right time for this idea, it will, by definition, spread. And it will spread internationally, perhaps first in the English-speaking nations, and then globally. Most of us are familiar with the notion of six degrees of separation; that anyone on the planet can be connected to anyone else in just six steps. The Mandate, if it spreads, will do so on this most powerful of all social networks. What happens as it goes international? And which country will hit the critical 25% figure first?

Chapter Eight
Transformation at National and Global Levels

If we are not to be condemned to oblivion, one country will be the first to hit the necessary social, political, and economic tipping points for change. This could happen within a year as elections take place. And, hopefully, this will happen before we hit the main global tipping points for environmental catastrophe. We are in a race of the tipping points.

I believe this change will happen first in one of our democracies, because it is harder to see how this transition can happen under an authoritarian regime. And, because this transition will threaten the dominant position of the financial markets, the markets will attack it by the withdrawal of financial assets and capital.

The only democracies that have the capability to withstand such a financial assault are those that have their own sovereign currency, as the UK does, and most other countries too. It will be a real challenge, but the markets cannot easily make a sovereign currency go bust. This is because of the monetary power of their central bank, in the UK the Bank of England. It can create money as required to keep the domestic economy functioning.

I have no idea which country will be the one to make the great transformation first. I think the UK is certainly a possibility. The discontents of neo-liberalism have gone further than in any other country in Europe. Arguably, this strengthens the motivation for change. But perhaps it will be a much smaller country which makes the jump first. I think of countries like Finland, or Iceland. Then again it may be Costa Rica or Bhutan. It's highly unpredictable. But if it is to happen at all, one country will be first. And this will be a hugely important historical step. Why?

Once one country makes this critical transition, it achieves a number of important things. It demonstrates feasibility, boosts social credibility, and becomes an inspiring role model. This lowers the threshold for other countries and increases the probability of them making the shift. As election cycles come due, more countries will be making the shift.

Perhaps there will be a flurry of such activity in the progressive Scandinavian countries, or those of South America. As long as there is a consistent pattern of growth, based on the continued spread of the Citizens' Mandate, the number of countries transitioning to the new political and economic systems of eco-social democracy will hit another important tipping point.

The global political tipping point

Initially these countries will align with each other and cooperate more. Whole economic blocs, perhaps such as Europe, will embrace the emerging new systems. Eventually they will hit a new international tipping point which will begin to change discourse and thinking at the global level. Call this the geopolitical tipping point.

Imagine that a majority of the G7 or the G20 countries have come on board with the new systems. Together they make up two-thirds of the world's population and 80% of the global economy. This gives them power to reshape the global governance system. But the question is, to what?

The transformation of global governance

First of all, to reshape global governance from what? Here's a quick overview of what passes for a global governance system. Most of it was set up around the end of World War II, with the Bretton Woods Agreement and is basically the management of global processes of commerce and finance in the absence of global government.

The main bodies include the United Nations. The UN is committed to maintaining international peace and security, maintaining friendly relations among nations, and promoting better living standards and human rights. The UN has done, and continues to do, a lot of good work on a tight budget $3.4 billion.

This is only 0.004% of global GDP in 2023. Of all the work it does, I will mention just one project because it bears so directly on the subject of this book.

The UN Sustainable Development Goals (SDGs)

These were adopted by the UN and all its 191 member states in 2015 with the intention of achieving them by 2030. There are 17 SDGs with 169 sub-targets. They emerged from a huge survey of around a million people from across the countries of the world. Here they are:

UN SDGs

1. No poverty
2. Zero hunger
3. Good health and wellbeing
4. Quality education
5. Gender equality
6. Clean water and sanitation
7. Affordable clean energy
8. Decent work and economic growth
9. Industry, innovation and infrastructure

10. Reduced inequality

11. Sustainable cities and communities

12. Responsible consumption and production

13. Climate action

14. Life below water

15. Life on land

16. Peace and justice strong institutions

17. Partnerships to achieve the goal

They fit well with the economic doughnut. They are all very good and worthy, apart perhaps from No 8 on unqualified economic growth. However, the SDGs are in many ways toothless, as UN resolutions are not legally binding.

The UN is run by nation states with one country having one vote. Five countries have a veto: China, France, Russia, the UK, and the USA. However, the agenda of most countries is dominated by the rich and powerful of those countries, the so-called 1%. In practice this is nearer to 1% of 1% of the 1%, which is 0.001%.

In addition to the UN, there are some 300 other bodies including these main ones:

World Health Organisation (WHO)

World Economic Forum (WEF)

International Monetary Fund (IMF)

World Bank

World Trade Organisation (WTO)

The financial and trade organisations above dominate the workings of the global economy and work primarily in service to the global neoliberal economic system. These organisations in turn tend to be dominated by the USA, the world's most powerful country, both economically and militarily. Many argue this is a hegemony, a dominance, of the world's economic systems by the USA. The dollar has been the world's main reserve currency for over 60 years, and this gives further power to the USA.

The Bretton Woods agreement was the last time that a new international monetary system was forged. This was motivated not just by World War II, but also by the major failures of the economic system previously, especially the Great Depression of the thirties. This failure of the economic system, with its massive financial inequalities, gave rise to fascism with its emphasis on authoritarianism, nationalism, elitism, hierarchy, and militarism. Does this sound slightly familiar?

The Great Recession of 2008 parallels this period and led to increases in inequality and so-called populist authoritarian parties and governments. Financial collapse was only averted by extensive 'quantitative easing'; effectively this is the creation of money to bail out the banks and boost the assets of the rich. And so the present neoliberal economic system staggers on for the moment. How may it change?

There are three main situations which may bring about structural change in the global economic system. First, another major financial disaster, one not amenable to the diminishing power of quantitative easing, could bring about the conditions for change. Next, runaway world wars could also do it; imagine the proliferation of the war in Ukraine, or China invading Taiwan. The third, and more hopeful option, would be the exponential growth of the Citizens' Mandate leading to a successful worldwide Citizens' Movement for Change.

The global economic systems

Before the conditions for change come about, we will need to have imagined the best alternatives and they will need to be widely talked about. Remember that quote from Milton Friedman:

"Only a crisis – actual or perceived – produces real change. When that crisis occurs, the actions that are taken depend on the ideas that are lying around... Our basic function (is) to develop alternatives to existing policies, to keep them alive and available until the politically impossible becomes the politically inevitable."

The question becomes, what are the best alternatives to the present global economic system? I don't know, and of course, the level of complexity can seem overwhelming, but here are a few ideas which I find quite compelling. Think of these as a starting point for discussion.

Currently, the world economic system is pegged to the American dollar, which is by far the world's biggest reserve currency. This has many advantages for the USA, but is not so good for the rest of the world.

The case for a global currency is being more commonly heard. This would replace the dollar. Keynes made a good case for this with E. F. Schumacher, of *Small Is Beautiful* fame, back in the forties around the time of the Bretton Woods agreement. They proposed an international currency which they called the 'bancor' to be used for settling international accounts.

To be issued by a central bank, it was designed to deal with the major problem of international trade. Some countries build up trade surpluses and others trade deficits. This tends to destabilise the system. Look at what happened to Greece in Europe, or to impoverished African countries: their economies collapsed.

Keynes's proposal was that when a country ran too far into deficit it would be required to devalue its currency to reduce imports. Too far into surplus and the currency would be required to appreciate to increase imports.

In addition, a bancor tax would be imposed on any country with a large trade imbalance. This would elegantly solve one of the main problems of international trade, the tendency to become unbalanced. This proposal was predictably overruled by the USA.

Perhaps an international currency would be a good function for a World Bank redesigned to be independent. The White House currently picks the head of the World Bank, and a redesign would change this. And perhaps we may also see a similarly redesigned independent IMF to finance countries on a more equitable basis than it currently does.

The IMF currently imposes neoliberal economic policies on countries in debt, causing privatisation of national welfare states, austerity, and effectively preventing states from running the most significant aspects of their own countries. You could call it neoliberal neo-colonisation.

Taken together, and independent of the USA, the World Bank and the IMF could be redesigned to operate in a similar way to that of the central bank and the commercial banks within a country. And, with GND policies, they would do this to the benefit of people and the environment. In principle, we can redesign the global economic system to be fit for purpose; a viable system, no less. It would certainly work better than the current system which is based mainly on 'horse trading between old men'.

Global wealth and income

But, again, where will the money come from? Here are a few figures on global wealth. The total estimated global wealth is $470 trillion (£390 trillion). This averages around $49,000 (£41,000) per person. Of this at least 10% is currently in tax havens, some $39 trillion. Of course, being hidden, this is notoriously hard to estimate, but one figure I saw recently was of $47 trillion.

Global income, based on world domestic product (WDP) is $80 trillion (£67 trillion). There is another measure of this based on the equivalent purchasing power of each dollar in different countries, called the purchasing power parity (PPP). This amounts to $130 trillion, (£108 trillion). The global average income per person is $10,000, (£8,000). In purchasing power equivalent this is $17,000 (£14,500) per person.

Paying for a global Green New Deal

To me, it looks like there is no shortage of wealth or income overall, it's just very unevenly distributed. How much would we need for a global GND? Most estimates I've seen run between 2-4% annually of total global income, between $1.6-3.6 trillion.

Bear in mind that this is not a cost, it's an investment; it will give good returns both financially and in human and environmental wellbeing. Also, remember Keynes's dictum: anything we can actually do, we can afford. International surveys are showing that around 75% of people would be happy to pay more for the wellbeing of people and the planet. I don't believe they need to.

Let's take the upper figure, 4%, or $3.6 trillion pa, and let's assume a 10 year global GND transition plan. That 4% figure is front-loaded; the heaviest investments are in the early years. As the GND moves towards full employment, tax revenues increase. Eventually the investment pays for itself.

In addition, the process of global transformation will decrease expenditure in unnecessary industries from planned obsolescence and marketing, through to military expenditure. The latter alone costs $2 trillion annually: taken together, that's most of our 2-4% right there. And fossil fuel subsidies run at around $1.25 trillion annually in direct government subsidies according to the World Bank. It puts agricultural subsidies at $540 billion, with 90% harmful and only 0.5% going to sustainable forms.

As an aside, the World Bank puts implicit fossil fuel subsidies, including waived taxes and the cost of environmental damage, at about $6 trillion annually, though a more recent (2023) and inclusive estimate by the World Bank puts this at $11 trillion.

Taking this into account, we can pretty much cover the investment cost without taking account of Modern Monetary Theory and our ability to create the money anyway. We could also just requisition the money from tax havens, which on its own would pay for some 7 years of the Global GND. The argument that we can't afford it just doesn't stand up. So what's stopping us? The political will, yet again.

The global political system

After the economic system, the other major aspect of global governance is the political side of it. Currently, this falls under the UN, which, as I pointed out earlier, is relatively toothless, because it is dominated by the agenda of the most economically powerful nation states and their veto rights. And they, in turn, are dominated by the vested interests. So, what would work better?

Here I look again for inspiration to Beer's Viable System Model (VSM), especially the 'here and now' organisation and management. Clearly some systems need to focus on the collective problems at the global level. A collective problem is any problem which can only be solved collectively. Breaking the planetary boundaries, as carbon dioxide emissions do, or the evasion of taxation by tax havens are both examples of these. They are so important for our survival that key decisions made on them would need to be legally binding.

At the other end of the spectrum are the majority of decisions that are best made at the lowest level possible. Think here of local council tax levels or planning permission for new buildings. The general principle of a viable system is that every decision is devolved to the lowest level that is practicable. This principle is known as subsidiarity.

Imagine the UN being redesigned along these lines as a viable system. It would be a bit like evolving a brain for global civilisation. Much work needed here I think…

But would a much-improved UN be the best for the job? After all, why give undue priority to the nation states? The nation state is a relatively recent phenomenon only going back around two or three centuries. Even passports have only been needed for travel since the First World War; before that you could travel freely anywhere in the world without one.

I could put tongue in cheek and argue for transnational corporations instead of, or as well as, countries. After all, 69 of the world's 100 biggest economic entities are now transnational corporations. But I won't. It's not the size of the economic entity that matters, the bottom line is it's people that ultimately matter, not money.

Instead of, or perhaps even as well as, the UN, we could have a different body. Rather than priority being given to economic power of nation states, priority could be given to people. This might be called the United People or the United Citizens. If the United Citizens had a global parliament of the same size as most parliaments, around 500 members, that would be one representative for a constituency of one and a half million people.

A system of this kind would shift power from wealth to people. And shifting power from wealth to people is what's needed. It is after all the power base of wealth that keeps us locked into the present system and the doom loop.

A best case scenario

The United Citizens could be run along the lines outlined earlier on the political systems within countries. This would include something like the multibody, sortition-based, system proposed by Terrill Bouricious. Citizens' Assemblies would then truly come into their own, with their ability to make high quality decisions without the corrupting influence of the vested interests.

This organic, and grassroots driven, new governance system would have the political power to change the global economic system. It would do this when we reach the global tipping point for political change, or when a major crisis, such as a devastating economic crash, hits us.

It's important that the best of these alternative systems are the ideas which are floating around at the time. Food for thought and food for conversations. Remember that question: what would your ideal society be like? Also up for discussion is: how would it be run?

The best of our alternative thinking provides a synthesis which would work vastly more effectively than the present system. As we've seen, our present system often comes down to no more than horse-trading between leaders of big nation states. I was struck by one critic who thought that if you had to design an economic system to be as destructive as possible, it would look remarkably like what we've got...

Imagine for a moment if, at the local, national, and global levels, we had governance and economic systems based on viable systems and truly fit for purpose. They would indeed form something like a nervous system for the planet, driven by the shared goal of optimising wellbeing for people and planet.

These would give new meaning to James Lovelock's Gaia Hypothesis. In this he proposed the idea that all organisms, and their inorganic surroundings on Earth, are closely integrated to form a single self-regulating complex system, maintaining the conditions for life on the planet. It is indeed remarkable that the conditions for life on our planet have been maintained as successfully as they have for some two billion years.

For the last few centuries, the economic systems have effectively been waging a war on Gaia, the living Earth. With these emerging new systems, humanity would re-align itself with Gaia. We may even see the emergence of an age of unprecedented wellbeing, a veritable renaissance, as we move into Kate Raworth's safe operating space for humanity. Perhaps we needed nothing less than a major planetary crisis to trigger such a major social transformation.

The main problem we face is turning things around before we activate the lethal environmental tipping points which still await us. The climate tipping points we know something of, but there are other environmental tipping points which we don't. It will be a close-run thing, but by adopting our best approaches this global transformation may well become humanity's finest hour.

If, in the worst case, we have already passed critical tipping points and face runaway climate change, we can rise to this challenge and plan for a rebuilding of civilisation on a smaller scale near the poles, which will be the only remaining habitable parts of the planet.

Whichever scenario we face, it seems clear that we, collectively, need to improve our systems thinking abilities.

Chapter Nine
Thinking in Systems for Systems That Work

About systems thinking

Let us return again to Sarah Smith's fundamental question from Chapter Two: "How do we so successfully and consistently produce results that nobody wants?" One answer, which I think is implicit throughout the approach I've taken, is this; we have a key blind spot. We are weak at perceiving how systems actually work. And the world, both natural and man-made, consists of systems. A couple of quotes here from Gregory Bateson, who was to my mind one of the most original thinkers of the last century:

"The major problems of the world are the result of the difference between how nature works and how people think."

"If you want to understand something, you have to understand how that thing thunk!"

I think both these quotes point to our weakness in systemic understanding. The skills of applied systems thinking are not yet widely known, yet they will form essential steps on our quest for systems that serve us better.

Systems thinking is based on building models of the systems of our natural and human-made worlds. These models are tested by practical application. Where they don't work the models are continually adjusted until they do. Systems thinking doesn't replace our traditional science-based worldview, rather it is complimentary.

I believe that systems thinking is still in its infancy. From its origins in cybernetics some 75 years ago, systems thinking has branched out into at least ten different sub-disciplines, each with their own strengths and weaknesses.

I don't believe you have to be an expert in systems thinking to make a difference. Just participating in the Mandate will do that. But those who lead and manage our political, economic, and organisational systems will need a better understanding of how they in fact work. The need for applied systems thinking will be enormous, and the interest in it is growing steadily so here is a little more about it.

Systems thinking overview

Systems thinking is a different way of thinking about the world, a different worldview, a different paradigm. In the West our predominant view of the world is scientific, and sees the world as being primarily mechanical in nature and based on the model of Newtonian physics. Traditional science has many strengths and has led to the development of the diverse technologies on which our civilisation is based.

Things have moved on since the days of Newton. Perhaps the first dent in this mechanistic worldview came with Darwin's work on evolution. The background variation in species led to a process of natural selection by which those best fitted to their environment survived and had more offspring. Over time this led to changes within each species, and to the emergence of distinct new species. This process of evolution, over some 3 billion years, led to the evolution of the natural world as we know it.

Newton's work on the laws of physics lends itself to a broadly mechanical worldview of relatively simple causes and predictable effects. Darwin's theory of evolution doesn't. There are multiple causes at work in complex organic systems where the effects are far from predictable. New behaviours emerge and new species emerge, often unpredictably. If you hit a billiard ball with another billiard ball you can predict the outcome pretty well. If you hit a dog with a billiard ball you can't! This may not be the best analogy, but it still makes the point well. The laws of the living world are different from the laws of the mechanical world.

The living world is characterised by complexity, and we are part of the living world of complexity. Some elements of systems thinking can be traced back to antiquity. I'm thinking here of the *Dao de Jing* by Lao Tsu which contains many elements of systems thinking. On page one we find:

"That which can be spoken of is not eternal. That which is named is not the eternal name."

The Newtonian worldview has left us with a legacy of thinking that the best way to understand something is to take it apart and understand the bits separately. Known as reductionism, this approach works well in some areas, but is a disaster in others. Our education system is based on reducing what is to be learned into different subject areas and understanding them separately. As a result, we nearly all suffer from this reductionist worldview.

The alternative is to look at the whole rather than the parts and try to understand how the parts interact with each other. The key to understanding the whole lies in understanding the relationship of the parts to each other and to the patterns of their behaviour, and how these patterns work together to create the behaviour of the whole system. This is not easy, as there is usually no simple understanding to be had. The best approach is to stay curious about what is really going on, then test out ideas to see what works in practice.

One general principle in systems thinking is that simple causation, one thing causing one effect, is far less common than multiple causation, where many things interact to cause one effect. Nor are these causes always one way. Causation can flow in both directions, feedback loops can both amplify or reduce a variable. Furthermore, you can have feedforward loops as well as feedback loops.

Another important principle is that history matters. Events depend on what has happened before. This is known as path dependence. The QWERTY keyboard we type on was developed in the 1870s to minimise jamming on mechanical typewriters. It became the norm, the path, which we are still dependent on to this day, because it's not practical to shift out of that norm. This is so even though many other keyboard layouts would be much easier to use.

Then there is the context or setting. The way that change happens and the future emerges, depends on the particular features and relationships of the local setting. One size does not fit all. This is why something that works in one setting won't always work in a different one without tailoring it to suit.

Also, complex systems can self-organise, and this gives rise to new features or behaviours emerging, which they do, as we have seen when tipping points are reached. The future does not always flow smoothly from the past, but nor is it chaotic. The world is neither random nor predictable, but somewhere in between.

Our conscious minds can only process a few variables at one time. Hence we are not well suited to the multi-variability of complex systems. So what are we to do? There are two main options. With a deep and broad experience base of any complex field, our unconscious minds seem able to map complex systems and we develop intuitions about how they work. The resulting maps will still need much testing in practice.

The other option is to build explicit models of the main elements of complex systems. These can be complex drawings showing the relationships of the parts to each other and to the whole. Or they can be computer models with the element of time added to make them dynamic. We looked at one example of this in Donella Meadows's *The Limits to Growth* models of human systems interacting with the Earth's natural systems.

Even if you are well motivated, it can take quite a while to get your head around some of the main elements of systems thinking. It is not something you 'get' such as learning enough knowledge to pass an exam. But over time you do improve at systems thinking.

One important element of this is unlearning, and returning to a point of knowing that you don't know. The only way you can find out something is to test it in practice. Ultimately systems thinking is an empirical approach, and is verified by experience rather than theory. It evaluates models or hypotheses in terms of their practical success. Where to start?

Donella Meadows

If you are a beginner and you'd just like to know more about systems thinking, a good place to start is to check out a couple of books by Donella Meadows. She was unusually gifted at both systems thinking and communicating it clearly. For an informal approach, I enjoyed *The Global Citizen*, a compilation of newspaper articles she wrote for the general public. However, *Thinking in Systems* is her bestselling classic primer on systems thinking, and should be required reading for all policymakers, leaders, and managers.

Levels of leverage

One of Donella Meadows's key insights was that different kinds of intervention in a system have different levels of leverage; changing some things will have a bigger effect than changing other things. Here are a few examples of the different levels of change we will need to get better at as we set forth on this greatest of all transformational journeys. It is taken from her list of the twelve main levels of intervention, from lowest to highest leverage.

She qualifies this list by pointing out that it is tentative, and the order is "slithery". There are exceptions to every item that can move it up or down the order of leverage. Also, the higher the leverage point, the more the system will resist changing it. For clarity I've left out the levels which are less important and harder to understand without having read *Thinking in Systems*. We'll move from the points of least leverage to those of the greatest.

Numbers

At the lowest point of leverage, and twelfth on her list, are numbers; constants and parameters such as subsidies or tax rates. It's not that these are unimportant. Indeed, shifting taxes and subsidies from 'goods' to 'bads' is a really important first step in GND proposals. The big advantage of changing taxes and subsidies is that they can be put in place relatively quickly and easily.

Stocks and flows

Tenth are what she calls stock and flow structures. Examples of these are our physical infrastructures for maintaining our energy stocks and flows. We need structures which store stocks of energy and structures to enable it to flow to where it is needed. We will have to largely rebuild these over a decade as we move from fossil fuels to sustainable energy sources. These are essential changes but are both capital intensive and slow to make.

Balancing feedback loops

Eighth comes balancing feedback loops, like the thermostat which switches off your heating when your home is warm enough. Important for these is the strength of the feedback compared to the impact they are trying to have. A protest movement can be thought of as a feedback loop, but has to become vast to effect change.

Reinforcing feedback loops

Seventh are reinforcing feedback loops. A reinforcing loop is when something feeds on itself; an example is when a microphone is too close to a speaker in a PA system. The mike picks up the sound from the speaker and sends it to the amp which boosts it and the system starts to scream.

One practical application of a reinforcing loop is that rich people pay less tax and enjoy higher rates of compound investment, so becoming richer. To them that hath shall be given… Another example of a reinforcing loop is the Citizens' Mandate, the more it is talked about, the more people become interested in it. As more people become interested, more people talk about it, and so on. The faster the spread rate, the more influential the movement becomes. And, as we've seen, with exponential growth it's only a matter of time before it hits the critical 25% figure.

Information flows

Sixth are information flows, which concern the structure of who or what has, or does not have, access to key information. A negative example is the lack of the information in the media which leads to a widespread public lack of understanding of the systemic nature of the crises we face. A positive example is when Citizens' Assemblies provide members with access to all the key expertise they need to adequately understand the topic on which they are to decide.

Another example is when, in the VSM, all operational systems and subsystems get the key information they need to work more effectively with all the other parts of the system. This book is itself an attempt to improve information flows by providing an understanding of the systemic nature of the crises we face, and some of the most promising pathways forward.

Self-organisation

Fourth on Donella Meadows's list is self-organisation. This is the remarkable ability to generate, apparently spontaneously, entirely new forms of system structure and patterns of thought and behaviour. Again, the Citizens' Mandate is an example of this, as also would be the new approaches that may emerge from the Mandate. Examples would be discussion and study groups as mentioned earlier, or spreading the Mandate in your local neighbourhood. The new forms of economic and political systems outlined earlier are also examples of self-organisation.

Goals

Third are goals, the aim or purpose of the system. Changing the purpose of the economic system from profit to wellbeing is the most obvious of these. Or changing the purpose of the political system from having controlling power, to a service to empower people; that is power with, rather than power over. When we change the purpose of a system we change what it does. This is one of the highest and most powerful places to effect change, but it is also a level which will be widely resisted. But it is not the highest level.

Paradigms

Second we have paradigms: the mind-set out of which the goals, structures, rules and parameters arise. Pause for thought here. We have shifted for the first time from the external world to our internal worlds. There is a very real sense in which everything we do in the external world is guided by our internal worlds. More on this later.

This is perhaps another reason why having conversations with friends about change is one of the most effective things you can do. Research shows that conversation with close friends is one of the most supportive environments for exploring, and sometimes changing, our core beliefs about the world. I'm reminded of a quote from Keynes:

"Practical men, who believe themselves to be quite exempt from any intellectual influences, are usually slaves to some defunct economists."

I'm pleased he apparently thought women were immune to this!

Our assumptions about the world are a part of our paradigms. In one of her articles Donella Meadows listed a few of the common misguided assumptions of society. She considered them to be both unsystematic and of incalculable harm. Here is a summary. As you look through, notice how they compare with your own assumptions.

- One cause produces one effect. All we must do is discover it and change it.
- All growth is good. There are no effective limits to growth.
- There is an 'away' to throw things to. When you have thrown it away, it is gone.
- Technology will solve any problem. Improvements will come from better technology, not better humanity.
- The future is to be predicted, not chosen or created. It is what happens to us.

- Any problem does not exist, or is not serious, until it is measured.
- If something is economic, it needs no further justification.
- Relationships between things are continuous, linear and non-delayed; feedback is accurate and timely; systems are manageable by simple cause-effect thinking.
- Results can be measured by effort expended. More spending on weapons means more security.
- Parts of systems are disconnected from each other. The economic system is separate from living systems. Optimising one part, like profit, doesn't sub-optimise other parts.
- Choices are either/or, not both/and.
- Possession of things is the source of happiness.
- Individuals cannot make a difference.
- People are basically greedy, bad, and not to be trusted. The exceptions prove the rule.
- The rational powers of the mind are superior to the intuitive and moral powers.
- Present systems are tolerable; alternative systems cannot help but be worse.
- We know what we are doing.

Donella Meadows believed the only way to deal with these assumptions of our culture is to keep questioning them. And now, finally, onto her first, and most powerful point of leverage. Prepare for a slight cognitive shock!

Transcending paradigms

Transcending paradigms, means going beyond our existing mental models of reality. What are we to make of this zen-like leverage point?

I consulted my Oxford dictionary. To transcend is to go beyond the range or limits of a conceptual sphere. A paradigm is a worldview underlying the theories and methodology of a particular subject. So, to transcend a paradigm is to go beyond a particular worldview. To boldly go into worldviews anew...

I think the main sense in which Donella Meadows means this, is to transcend our current ideologies. Again, a reminder on ideology, my dictionary defines an ideology as a system of ideas or ideals which form the basis of economic or political theory and policy. What is the currently dominant system of ideas or ideals? The neoliberal economic system. This is what we must transcend.

How do we do this? One reflection at a time, one conversation at a time. What are we to replace it with? This is for you to decide. In a sense, one of the main purposes of writing this book is to provide you with a wealth of the best alternatives to replace our current ideology.

I am unable to summarise it all in a neat sentence because it's too big and too complex. But if there is a common purpose it is wellbeing; the ultimate metric of eudemony, a flourishing wellbeing for all.

The key insight I take away from this is that all ideologies are inherently limited and filled with contradictions and undecidable propositions. If this is so, where do we go? What is the ultimate non-ideological position?

Beyond ideologies

I think the only answer we are left with is radical pragmatism. Pragmatism is an approach that evaluates theories, beliefs, or policies in terms of their success or practical application. It has a strong basis in different fields. In the wisdom traditions of the world, knowing that you don't know is the beginning of wisdom. This sits well with most systems thinking approaches in which all assumptions and all models are tentative; they are not the truth.

According to Karl Popper, one of the greatest philosophers of science of the twentieth century, a theory in the empirical sciences can never be proven. It can only be falsified with experiments. Science cannot prove, it can only disprove. In a very real sense, all scientific knowledge is hypothetical or provisional.

If global transformation towards systems that work better is going to come, then more of us are going to be applying these pragmatic systems thinking skills. If you want to dig deeper in the world of systems thinking, where do you go next? Here are a few suggestions to get you started.

A comprehensive overview – Critical Systems Thinking

If you are seriously interested in systems thinking and how to apply it, or perhaps are someone in a position of influence in a significant organisation, then what is the best and most comprehensive source to go for? I think Michael Jackson's *Critical Systems Thinking* does the job well and is up to date (2019). Be warned, it is not for the faint of heart or mind! It runs to 645 pages of dense small print.

Of particular importance is his System of Systems Methodologies which maps each of the systems models according to their strengths onto a grid. This grid runs from simple systems to complex ones on one dimension, and from single to multiple and then coercive stakeholders on the other. He covers all of this in his course on Critical Systems Thinking.

The chapter I found most inspiring is his last one on Critical Systems Practice. Here he takes Critical Systems Theory and describes its practical application. This gets pretty complex with the simultaneous application of multiple methodologies, multi-methodology as it is called. This is particularly true since different methodologies have both different assumptions and different underlying paradigms.

However, applied Critical Systems Thinking can be remarkably effective at successfully transforming organisations. And, as far as we are concerned, that is the holy grail! It gives us a way of achieving the changes we want and need in our organisations if we are to have a future worth having.

I have chosen five of what I consider to be the most useful of the ten main approaches to systems thinking to explore in a bit more depth below.

The Viable Systems Model and Team Syntegrity

I am no expert on all the different approaches to systems thinking, but I've been most drawn to Stafford Beer's Viable Systems Model, as you will have noticed. We explored this in some depth at the beginning of Chapter Five. Also important is Stafford's 'Team Syntegrity', a powerful process for effective collective decision making, described in his book *Beyond Dispute: The Invention of Team Syntegrity*.

Soft Systems Methodology

I also found Peter Checkland's book *Soft Systems Methodology* useful. He developed this on the basis of 10 years' research. It's a way to model business processes based more on the skills of personal interaction, often a weakness in applied systems thinking, and can be used for general problem solving and managing organisational change.

The Fifth Discipline

Peter Senge, a systems thinker at MIT, wrote a best seller in 1990 *The Fifth Discipline* which outlined systems archetypes. A systems archetype is a common pattern of system behaviour. It is a useful way to introduce people to recognising different patterns of systems behaviour in practice. Here are a couple of examples. 'Success to the Successful', think Elon Musk, one of the world's richest men; the more money you have, the easier it is to make money. Or 'Escalation'. Here, where two sides are competing, there is every incentive to up the ante. Classic examples include the nuclear arms race that the USA and the then USSR got stuck in, or a couple in an antagonistic divorce.

The Vanguard Method

Another approach is the Vanguard Method, developed by John Seddon, an occupational psychologist, and outlined in his book *The Whitehall Effect*. He is critical of what he calls the industrialization of public services using command and control, targets, incentives, and inspections. He says, "Politicians don't know much about management." And he gives a damning account of the "industrialization of public services" in the UK since the time of Thatcher, and based on targets. The Vanguard Method takes a different, and more humane, management-savvy approach based on the quality control movement of Toyota and others which led to their domination of car manufacturing. If adopted by government services, the evidence is that it would be one of the most effective ways of making public services work better for most people.

Complexity Theory

One of my systems thinking favourites is complexity theory. Whether we like it or not, the world is complex, and this approach does justice to this. As Hamlet said:

"There are more things in heaven and Earth, Horatio, than are dreamt of in your philosophy."

Most of my systems thinking overview at the start of this chapter is drawn from complexity theory, so I won't repeat it here. But I will refer you to the book I most like in this field: *Embracing Complexity –*

Strategic Perspectives for an Age of Turbulence by Jean Boulton, Peter Allen, and Cliff Bowman. It is well written and outlines the complexity worldview which is closer to our lived experience than the mechanistic worldview with its command-and-control style organisations. Their book serves well as an intermediate level introduction to systems thinking.

Culture change

As far as I know, there is no systems thinking discipline which focusses exclusively on culture change, though some touch on it. This is a shame. It is an area I specialised in precisely because it is one which organisations find so difficult. There's a saying, "Culture eats strategy for breakfast." I think you get the idea. I enjoyed the challenge and worked in the field for 30 years. Eventually I got to the level of being able to facilitate change with full qualitative and quantitative evidence of success. Perhaps this is a field ripe for development.

Nora Bateson

I can't resist mentioning *Small Arcs of Larger Circles* by Nora Bateson, Gregory Bateson's daughter. Although I've quoted from Gregory Bateson earlier, I haven't introduced him. He was one of the most influential and original English thinkers of the twentieth century, an anthropologist, scientist, linguist, semiotician and cyberneticist. Two of his books, *Steps to an Ecology of Mind* and *Mind and Nature* profoundly influenced my thinking and that of this book.

His daughter Nora Bateson follows in his footsteps and *Small Arcs of Larger Circles* is one of the most profound and enjoyable books I've read recently, although not included in Jackson's *Critical Systems Thinking*. In her book she weaves together applied systems thinking and complexity theory with our embodied aesthetic experience.

It is a lush garden of densely interconnected ideas and experiences growing in a framework of essays, philosophy, and poetry. And it introduces you to some of her leading-edge work on warm data, trans-contextual learning and symmathesy, which I won't even attempt to explain, but if you like original thinking, and want a taste of where applied systems thinking may be heading, you'll like her book.

In summary

Systems thinking is a worldview I heartily commend if you want to improve your understanding of how the world really works. This is very different to the myths of the consensus reality on which we have been brought up, and in which we currently live. Thinking systemically is based on building models of reality and testing them in practice. If they don't fit reality, systemic thinking keeps you changing the model until it fits better with how the world actually works, by a process of successive approximation.

If this kind of thinking were to become more common and widespread, it would have a massive impact on the ills of the human made world. Most of our ills are created by our significantly dysfunctional systems, from governance, through economics, right down to our businesses and other organisations. Imagine how, with the veil lifting from our blind spot on how systems actually work, and with progressive change expanding, we would see a growing improvement in the quality of our lives in all areas.

Where does this exploration of systems thinking leave us? Secure in the knowledge that we know nothing, we are freed from the shackles of obsolete ideologies and so can explore all possibilities.

There is no law in science or elsewhere which prevents us from creating a world which, seen from our present viewpoint, would be relatively utopian; or more accurately, eutopian. Utopia, based on the

Greek, literally translates as no place. Eutopia, were it a word (it's not yet in my dictionary), translates as good place.

Perhaps this is as good a place as any to end this chapter, pondering the eutopian possibilities of the future...

In the next chapter, we go back and revisit our current human predicament and the range of potentially overwhelming crises we faced in the first chapter. Are we really able to resolve our apparently overwhelming problems? How would these crises look different in a world transformed?

Chapter Ten
The Human Predicament Revisited

In this chapter, I'll assume that the Mandate, or something that can do the same job, succeeds in transforming our political and economic systems so they can successfully take on the major challenges we face. I'll take each in turn and assess the difference a successful transformation will make.

The planetary boundaries

We'll take our biggest problems first, starting with the six planetary boundaries in which we are already outside the safe zone. We'll take them in order of risk as assessed by the Stockholm Resilience Centre.

Novel Entities

We have seen that 10 million tons of an estimated 350,000 different chemical pollutants are released into the environment each year. This is a massive issue. Where do we start? We don't even know the effects of most of these pollutants as some estimates say well under 1% has been tested.

I believe resolving this issue will be a major growth area. We will need to develop rigorous testing of the effects, and rank all pollutants in order of the damage they do. We will also need to ban the production of chemicals for which there is no real necessity and use only the safest ones which meet our real needs. The circular economy will grow, and recycle as many of these as possible.

First, we need the ten-year transition plan to move us to a material economy that is sustainable in the long term. In other words, we're aiming for zero pollution. You can argue that this is theoretically impossible, but the closer we can get the better. It's exactly the kind of challenge that our transformed economic and political systems will be designed to deal with. We might invent an economic measure for generalised pollution productivity, GPPRO.

As with CO_2 pollution, after stabilisation of pollutants, there comes drawdown. This is the process of withdrawing pollutants from the environment. We have already discovered microorganisms that live off some plastics, however this field is still in its infancy. We can expect the research effort in this area to proliferate and boom. With the developments in biotechnology, nanotechnology and artificial intelligence combined, and massively funded, in ten years' time we will have made more progress than seems currently conceivable.

Biosphere Integrity

The loss of biodiversity, the reduction in the biomass and number of species, threatens us in many ways. The ultimate threat is the collapse of the biosphere, the living world. Because we depend on the biosphere, this is an existential threat for human civilisation.

The main culprit here is increasing our land use, mainly for agriculture. In the transformation process, this is reversed. As we eat less meat, we use less land. As we transit from agribusiness to small intensively managed farms, we produce more food on less land. And as I mentioned in the Introduction, there is one new type of technology in the pipeline which promises to be a game changer.

This only came to my attention recently when reading George Monbiot's 2022 book, *Regenesis: Feeding the World Without Devouring the Planet*. This outlines how we can produce more food with less land while locking more CO_2 in the soil. But one chapter really captured my imagination.

Monbiot describes the pioneering work of Pasi Vainikka in Helsinki, with his start-up company Solar Foods. Pasi Vainikka has developed a way of growing a particular soil bacterium in brewing tanks. Not just any soil bacterium, but one which draws its energy from hydrogen; it's a hydrogen-oxygenating bacterium. He feeds it with hydrogen split from water by hydrolysis and the energy for this comes from solar panels. The bacteria are 60% high quality protein and are used to make a tasty protein rich flour called Solein. There may be other bacteria we can cultivate that can do an even better job.

So far, so good. The thing that made me sit up and really pay attention was this. The process uses 45 times less land than soya, our most protein intensive crop, uses to produce the same amount of protein. That's just 2% of the land area! If wind power were used, instead of solar, this figure drops to 0.4%! This really does change everything. Why?

About 70% of our farmland is used to produce either animals for protein, or food-stock for animals. With this one step we can free up two-thirds of our farmland. Suddenly, rewilding at scale becomes feasible. Edward Wilson in his book, *Half-Earth: Our Planet's Fight for Life*, proposes an achievable plan to save our imperilled biosphere by devoting half the Earth's surface to nature. With global transformation, this would be well under way in ten years.

Biogeochemical Flows

According to the Stockholm Resilience Centre, biogeochemical flows are up there with biosphere integrity as one of our major risk areas. The main culprit here is nitrogen, closely followed by phosphorus.

They poison our waters with nitrates and phosphates, and this is caused mainly by the agribusiness-for-profit system.

Changing the key drivers for the business world, as outlined earlier, undermines the present agricultural business model, and causes a rapid transition to all the more sustainable forms of agriculture. Apart from the brewing of key soil bacteria mentioned above, there is a huge range of practices being developed around the world. To name but a few:

- Agroforestry and food forests
- Small scale intensive production
- Polycultures and crop rotation
- Perennial vegetable and cereal crops
- Permaculture
- Organic farming and horticulture
- Natural animal raising
- Natural pest management

One of the key features which all sustainable forms of agriculture have in common is using natural fertility rather than artificial fertilisers like nitrogen and phosphorus. It's likely that two key measures of the success of future farms will be nitrogen productivity, NIPRO, and phosphorus productivity, PHOPRO, mentioned in Chapter Six. All these different measures together will enable us to reverse the problem of biogeochemical flows.

Land-system Change

In this planetary boundary we are also currently outside the safe zone. However, the solutions to the climate crisis, biosphere integrity and biogeochemical flows above, all involve reversing the problematic patterns of land use. In resolving these, we also resolve the problems of land-system change and, as we've seen, enable half the land area of the planet to be returned to nature.

This all happens because the global transformation approach is not about treating surface symptoms. It is about looking for the underlying systemic causes of the different symptoms. In changing the systems that cause the problems, we get synergistic gains between the solutions; that is, resolving one issue makes it easier to resolve the other ones because the combined effects are greater than the sum of their parts.

Climate Change

I started this book with a look at the climate crisis, possibly the biggest single existential threat that human civilisation has ever faced. If the Citizens' Mandate lifts off in anything like the way it could, how might our situation look in a decade's time?

The great global transformation will have largely shut down all the main human-made sources of global greenhouse emissions. A massive project will be underway to draw down carbon dioxide. The three main strands of this project are: massive reforestation and afforestation, transforming agriculture to store more carbon in the soil, and direct carbon capture drawdown technologies. There will be others.

Project Drawdown was described in 2013 by Paul Hawken in his book, *Drawdown: The Most Comprehensive Plan Ever Proposed to Reverse Global Warming*. It brings together some 200 experts to evaluate 80 technologies and practices. The results shocked even these experts. Combined, these 80 solutions would eliminate one trillion tons of CO_2 from the atmosphere by 2050. This alone is enough to prevent the dangerous climate tipping points of 2°C. And these solutions would cost less than business-as-usual, and provide more jobs. We will need other solutions as well to achieve 1.5°C.

Before getting carried away on a wave of optimism, bear in mind that we don't know which specific tipping points may come into action between now, 1.2°C, and then, 2.0°C; nor whether these will trigger runaway climate change. That's why it's better to aim to limit the temperature increase to only 1.5°C as a matter of urgency. All is in play, and will remain so for the foreseeable future.

However, in principle we know how to combat climate change, we can afford it, and with the political will, helped by yourself and many others, we can do it.

Freshwater Change

As we start to stabilise the planetary climate we will begin to improve the availability of fresh water. One of the biggest influences will be reducing and transforming our agricultural practices.

Increased resource wars are one main risk of growing water shortages. With the great transformation, more countries will become more democratic. Democracies start fewer wars than authoritarian and autocratic regimes. With transformation, so-called democracies will become more truly democratic, and autocracies will flip to become democratic. Within the ten-year timescale of the great transformation we can look forward to something remarkable: the end of war and the beginning of worldwide peace.

In the meantime, together with climate change, fresh water scarcity is a growing feature of life for many. In the short-term, smart metering, with no charge up to an average level of use, can alleviate the problem. But there's a more fundamental difficulty. There are some places that are not suitable for human habitation because of chronic water shortage, and these areas are growing.

As we've seen, half the world's population currently live in areas of water shortage for at least one month per year. While desalination plants can help some near the sea, for others, the solution is a longer term one. We will need to stop building in water-scarce areas which happen to be profitable in the short-term. However, driven by turning around both the climate problem and agricultural practices, overall water scarcity will be decreasing.

So far, we've looked at the six planetary boundaries where we are already outside the safe operating space. Next, we go onto those where we are arguably still within the safe operating space, but rapidly getting closer to the danger zone. These are, again, in order of danger.

Ocean Acidification

This threatens the integrity of the ecosystems of our oceans. The fundamental cause is the increasing levels of CO_2 because the oceans, along with soil, act as a main sink for atmospheric CO_2. The fundamental solution is to stop burning fossil fuels and start drawing down CO_2 from the atmosphere. When we get to the point of drawing down more CO_2 than we release, net zero, this begins to reverse ocean acidification. It may well take more than ten years to get to this point, but it will work in the long term.

Atmospheric Aerosol Loading

Aerosol loading is the amount of very small particles of solid or liquid in the air which we breathe. Although this is increasing as the current economy continues to grow, aerosol loading will stabilise as the material sectors of the economy stabilise, then reduce. The rapid switch away from fossil fuels will have a major positive impact on this.

As materials are better recycled within circular economies, aerosol loading will drop. And aerosol productivity measures, AERPRO, will accelerate this. One of the most effective first steps in terms of saving lives will be faster replacement of cooking on open stoves in the Global South with sustainable alternatives.

Stratospheric Ozone Depletion

The Montreal Protocol agreed in 1987 is an encouraging success story. 99% of ozone producing chemicals is no longer being produced. Ozone levels are expected to recover by 2040 to 1980 levels, before the ozone hole appeared. This case history gives us hope that humanity can act cooperatively and effectively in the face of imminent danger.

Planetary boundaries summary

Having had a look at all the risks posed by the boundaries of the planet and explored how they are mainly resolved in a post-transformation world, I'm guessing you find yourself feeling more hopeful about our shared future. Now, let's do the same for the other risks we looked at in the first chapter. For each we'll examine whether our global transformation improves our prospects or not, and we'll start with the natural risks.

Natural risks

These are the main risks apart from all the man-made ones, which are by far the biggest. In two of the three, it does look as though there is something we can do to mitigate these risks.

Asteroid or comet collisions

If you remember, a hit by an asteroid of 1 kilometre diameter causes severe disruption on a global scale. The chance of this in the next century is less than one in 120,000. But a strike by an asteroid of 10 kilometres would create a prolonged nuclear winter which would end human civilisation and cause mass species extinctions. However, since the probability is less than one in 250 million, this is not a case for great concern.

What is within our power to do? NASA in the USA has already done much research on this, which is how we know the figures. We have already started experimenting with nudging asteroids out of potential collision courses. There is an optimum spend level on extending this type of research internationally, and a balance to be struck on this expenditure versus the expenditure on all the other dangers. This decision, like so many others, will be best made by governance systems based on Citizens' Assemblies.

Supervolcano eruptions

A supervolcanic eruption does about the same amount of damage as a 1 kilometre asteroid strike. With a chance of one in 800 per century the risk is higher than for steroid strikes and my guess is that proportionately more funding will go into this. But volcanic eruptions aren't predictable I hear you say...

The first daily weather forecast was published in the UK in 1861 in The Times, based on the research of an officer in the Royal Navy, Francis Beaufort, and his protégé Robert FitzRoy. Before then, the weather wasn't scientifically predictable. We're at about that stage now with predicting eruptions; we're just beginning.

With research and funding, we can develop dynamic simulations of the underground systems of rock and magma and the quality of the predictions will improve. This will save many lives. But it will not necessarily completely solve the core (pardon the pun) problem. One day perhaps. Maybe there are some risks we just need to learn to live with.

Stellar explosions

Yes, they're possible, and out of our control, but with a chance of only one in several million, we're reaching diminishing returns. Remember Toby Ord's estimate of the combined risk of all natural disasters was less than 0.05% per annum. These risks are dwarfed by the human caused risks which are over 1,000 times more likely. So let's take a look at the other risks in our post-transformation world.

Anthropogenic risks

Again, these are the directly human-caused risks.

Global thermonuclear war

The big one. We can't estimate the probabilities, but they increase in proportion to geopolitical tensions. Our rapid transition to more truly democratic countries reduces the risk of wars in general, and that directly reduces the risk of nuclear war. If, with a democratic global governance system, we end war within a decade, one major gain of the peace dividend will finally be the dismantling of all weapons of nuclear destruction. Amen.

Overpopulation

Yes, we're overpopulated; we're currently living off 1.75 Earths. But that's only because our levels of material consumption are so high. As we move towards material sufficiency, whilst optimising quality of life, we will move towards living off only one Earth.

The great transformation can achieve this, and it will reduce the birth rate faster than currently. We may stabilise at nine, or maybe ten, million people. After that will come a gradual shrinking of the human population towards a self-determined optimum level. Overpopulation is not in itself a major risk.

Other future risks

As well as the above, there are the other main risks we face.

Pandemics

These are high risk for us. I read recently of bird flu, an H5N1 virus, having jumped species to a small number of people with a 50% fatality rate. It hasn't yet spread from person to person. But interpersonal spreading may be only a few mutations away. Scary! Pandemics remain a significant danger; what then are we to do?

This is another area where we need to rapidly accelerate both our preventative measures and our research and development funding. One fertile field is the exploitation of bacteriophages, viruses that live off bacteria, to take out bacterial diseases. And there has been a recent discovery of virophages, viruses that live on other viruses and could be developed to cope with any viral pandemic such as Covid.

Applied research on areas like these, using leading-edge genetic and biochemical technologies driven by AI, offer huge potential. Simultaneously, we need to ramp up preventive measures to reduce the probabilities of disease species jumping to humans. These include outlawing bush-meat and the intensive breeding of animals in conditions which foster diseases.

And finally, having learned from Covid, we need to be thoroughly prepared and equipped in advance. Taiwan has demonstrated what is possible with massive online democracy, so we now know what to do. There is no excuse when the next pandemic hits. By combining all these different measures, we can massively reduce our vulnerability to pandemics.

Artificial intelligence

The two main risks here, which I mentioned in the first chapter, are widespread job losses and takeover by an artificial general intelligence

(AGI). AIs taking over jobs is the easier of the two to deal with. The job creation abilities of the GND basically take care of it, with negative income tax acting as a backstop. We will be able to spend more time in meaningful work and the AIs can have what David Graeber called the 'bullshit jobs', in his book of that name, *Bullshit Jobs: The Rise of Pointless Work, and What We Can Do About It.*

AGI is trickier, especially with regard to weapons applications. I suspect it will follow a similar path to chemical and biological weapons. The specialists in the field have spoken up about the dangers, leading to international agreements and regulations. In the midst of the great transformation this should happen much faster and much more effectively. And of course, managed for the benefit of all, AGIs could be a massive boon for humanity; you could write a book on that alone.

Dystopian scenarios

The kind of dystopian scenarios on which I've focussed, are centred on authoritarian leaders of the populist right. This threat happens mainly at the level of the nation state and there are two main dangers. First, the authoritarian mindset is predisposed against most of the forms of progress we need to see, from dealing with the climate crisis on through the more progressive agenda of the GND and global transformation. Second, there is a strong case to be made that the authoritarian mind, when in a position of power, is the fundamental cause of most wars.

How real is this problem? Well, one survey puts the percentage of countries that are run by authoritarian regimes at 38%, by hybrid regimes at 18%, by flawed democracies at 37%, leaving just 7% to qualify as real democracies. Perhaps all a bit subjective, but it gives an indication.

Another estimate in 2017 put 57% of countries as democracies of some type, of these 28% had elements of democracy and autocracy, while only13% of countries were autocracies. There is quite a wide range of views out there!

Broadly speaking the proportion of governments which are democracies has been steadily increasing since the mid-seventies. The processes of global transformation which we have been looking at will vastly accelerate that. It is possible that eventually all countries will become more truly democratic along the lines we've been exploring.

However, as social tensions increase, which they are currently doing, we are seeing a movement towards more authoritarian and populist governments. We saw the effects of this in the thirties and it led to world war.

This time around we are again seeing the growth of the authoritarian right in politics. Their playbook strategy is to use wealth and media influence to blame vulnerable minorities, for example by stirring up xenophobia, "an invasion of immigrants". At the same time, they increase inequality, support fossil fuel use, and disseminate climate change denial.

Of course, increasing fossil fuel use means worsening climate disruption and displacing more people from their homes and from their countries. We already have an estimated 600 million people displaced by climate change. As the numbers grow, the right will ramp up their attack on immigrant invasion, a vicious positive feedback loop. It well may be that fighting Earth systems collapse, and fighting the rise of the far right, are two sides of the same coin. The rise of authoritarian right-wing leaders is the dystopian threat writ large. What is the best way to tackle this very real problem?

Ultimately, I believe that making countries more democratic, in the ways I've outlined, is by far the most effective way of addressing the dystopian threat.

The dystopian threat adds urgency to the tasks in front of us, but it can also motivate each of us to take constructive action on those things which are within our power to influence. You can join the movements for change which align best with your views and do what you can to minimise the environmental damage of your lifestyle whilst optimising your quality of life. And, of course, you know what I'm going to say next... you can participate in the Citizens' Mandate, one of the most effective things that you can do, and with the diverse citizens' movements which I believe will emerge from the Mandate process.

A last thought on this threat; the dynamic computer simulations that the book *Earth for All* is based on, factor in social tension as one of the key variables, and all of its five main proposals target social tensions very effectively. Decreasing them decreases the risks of authoritarian and dystopian governments. The dystopian threat is perhaps one of the biggest we face, but the democratic processes of global transformation are well able to minimise this threat.

Additional risks

There are two other possible threats which I mentioned. They are threats from emerging technologies such as nanotechnology or biotechnology. The answers here are similar to those for AI. With optimised governance systems we can minimise the chance of harm though practical wisdom in our regulation systems. We can optimise the considerable benefits, most of which are yet to be imagined.

ET

Finally, will extra-terrestrials take us over? It's a common theme in dystopian fiction and films but probably speaks more to the fears of our collective unconscious than to any reality. Feel free to worry about this one if you'd like to, but personally I don't find these fears very compelling. Why?

Any extra-terrestrial civilisations that are still out there will have had to pass through their equivalent of the species wisdom test which we are currently undergoing. Perhaps one of the reasons why SETI, the search for extra-terrestrial intelligence, has not found other intelligent lifeforms yet is that the wisdom test is a hard one, and most fail. This pithy poem points to the key dilemma.

Homo Sapiens

On a planet called Earth the evolutionary game
Created a species with this self-chosen name.
An unfortunate misnomer, they were clever not wise
And evolution decreed their autogenic demise.

There is a very real sense in which the race is on between our cleverness and our wisdom.

Alien life forms will have had to develop the wisdom to survive the destructive forces that young civilisations face and to thrive in the long term. The chances are they would probably also have the wisdom to leave us alone to go through our wisdom testing stage. I rather like the idea that in a decade or so, assuming we pass, they'll show up, say hello, and welcome us to the intergalactic federation…

Or have I watched too much Star Trek? Anyway, it is nearly time to boldly go and explore frontiers anew.

But before we do, let's just summarise this important chapter on how our threats look in the face of an effective global transformation.

Summary of the threats revisited

It's worth revisiting the key points here to boost our levels of hope and to remember what we are aiming for.

Planetary boundaries

These are probably the most obvious and present danger. However, because these risks are all caused by the dysfunctions of our human systems, they can all be resolved by changing our systems to ones which work as we would wish them to. The issues are those of scale and timescale.

Changing our political and economic systems is an issue of conceptual scale, but can in principle be done with powerful interventions like the Mandate, with massive general support, and the emergence of a movement combining all movements for change. This may be a Citizens' Movement for Change or something else, and could happen on a global scale within five years, this being the most common length of election cycles.

Changing our global energy and materials infrastructures will be the biggest single project humanity has even attempted. In principle it is feasible, but the timescale involved is probably in the order of ten years. This assumes we collectively wake up and go for it on a war footing, only more.

Adding the election cycle time of five years to the infrastructure replacement time estimate of ten years, then changing our political, economic and infrastructure systems could take some fifteen years. This falls within the timescale which we probably still have to make these changes before the main collapse happens.

Natural risks

We have always faced the possibility of asteroid strikes, volcanic eruptions, and other natural disasters, and always will. Yet there is much we can do to anticipate and ameliorate these. The risks are low compared to the others we face, and we can reduce them to a minimal level.

Anthropogenic and other risks

These risks are more subjective and harder to quantify. The big ones which concern me most are the dystopian scenarios of increasing authoritarian rule which increase human misery and ecological damage, escalating warfare leading to nuclear warfare, and pandemics.

Of these, pandemics are perhaps the simplest to resolve. We know the capabilities we need to develop and how to develop them. Warfare and the growth of authoritarian rule are more complex, but the direction of positive travel is clear. We must do all in our power to foster a massively enhanced level of democratic governance. And we have the know-how to do this. Only truly democratic governance has the capability of reducing the forces of populist authoritarian rule, and reducing the probability of warfare, both conventional and nuclear.

The overall outlook

This is potentially good, but only if we go all out for the kind of global transformation project that I've attempted to map here. Without this, we are probably doomed.

For this type of transformation to work, all we need is enough people to be sufficiently dissatisfied with the present situation to join together in speaking out. The Citizens' Mandate for Change provides a way of doing this.

We can speak out to give voice individually and collectively to what we don't want, what we do want, and how to get there. I believe this is necessary and sufficient to trigger the process of breaking out of our locked-in systems and changing the world; a bold claim. It is of course for you to decide, and if you do believe it is possible, to act on it.

Your thinking is very much the subject of the next chapter.

Chapter Eleven
Back to You

Our explorations so far have been mainly about matters of the external world. And, of course, what goes on in the outer world matters hugely. But it is not all that matters. There is an inner world too, a world in which you simultaneously live, your inner world of subjective experience.

For those who are interested in change there is a tendency to focus more on change either in the outer world or in the inner world. Few of us are in balance on this. Change in the outer world focuses on areas such as politics, protest or local alternatives, but without inner change this puts wellbeing at risk and ultimately leads to exhaustion and burnout. Change in the inner world takes the form of personal or spiritual development and growth, but unless there is external change we will not escape impending crises.

What works best is a balance of both worlds. The majority tend to favour one over the other. Which way do you lean? And how may you achieve a more optimal balance? In this chapter we will, unusually for a book of this kind, take a closer look at the inner world.

Your inner world matters, and here are a few reasons why. Our outer world is ultimately created by our inner worlds and our assumptions are the basis of both. This is why they are fundamental to change. Ignoring the workings of your inner world is the ultimate cause of despair, hopelessness, and burnout. Embracing your inner world is the pathway to evolving yourself and enhancing your quality of life, especially in adverse circumstances.

I think we are often as blind to the systemic workings of our inner worlds as we are to the systemic workings of the outer world. Many people naively think they live in the 'real world', by which they mean the external world. However, we don't, in the following sense.

Constructing the world

Imagine looking at a rose. Neuroscience shows that it takes a fraction of a second for the light hitting your retina to be transformed by your visual cortex into an internal representation of the rose, which is unconsciously projected out so you 'see' the rose out there in the external world. Our eyes are, in this respect, not like a camera. With the visual cortex we literally construct what we see.

As with our eyes, so with our other main senses; we construct the world internally and it is made up of our inner representations. In a very real sense, the world we live in is not the real world, but our representations of it. This is known as radical constructivism and is well explored in *The Invented Reality* edited by the psychologist Paul Watzlawick. As Albert Einstein once quipped:

"Reality is merely an illusion, albeit a very persistent one."

For most practical matters this exploration of epistemology – how we know what we know – is relatively unimportant. You can continue to enjoy looking at roses, and smelling them too. However, there are two areas where our construction of reality is significant.

The first is in our social worlds. Our agreed social reality, the so-called consensus reality, is also constructed, but by social agreement. As we've seen, once the Earth was flat, now it is not. Once climate change didn't exist, now it does, well, for most of us anyway. Neoliberal capitalism runs the world now, but in the future…?

The second area where it is significant is in our internal worlds. Our internal representations, thoughts, feelings, and beliefs often get snarled up and we experience emotional pain. At the other end of the spectrum they can flow sublimely well and we experience profound wellbeing, bliss even. Most of the time, for most of us, they vary around the middle ground. A good way of thinking about this is that we each experience varying 'emotional weather'.

Also, on matters emotional, do remember that our poor brains have only evolved very recently in evolutionary terms. They probably have a lot of design glitches still built in. Chronic depression, for example, may be a design glitch, although there is a theory that it's an adaptation to long cold winters. Maybe.

In this book so far, we've looked at the biggest crises we collectively face and sought out the most promising ways forward, with wellbeing for all as our lodestone. In this chapter I want to focus inwards, on how these issues may be affecting you, and how to achieve personal wellbeing in the face of them.

Facing the threats

If you're reading this book, then the chances are that you, like the majority, are very concerned about where we seem to be headed. What is the best way to respond to this?

Start by acknowledging the threats, for they are real. The appropriate response is to then do what is within your power to usefully engage with them. Of course, participating in the Citizens' Mandate is one of the most effective things which is within your power to do. There are many other actions you can take, and we'll be looking at these in more depth in Chapter Twelve.

As long as you are doing what truly motivates you, this seems to free up the energy absorbed by the anxiety about what we are facing, and by our cognitive dissonance. Cognitive dissonance is the perception of contradictory information and the mental and emotional toll it takes. For example, you know that adding to the burden of carbon dioxide is part of the problem; yet you have a house to heat, and you need to drive, or you want a holiday in sunnier climes.

Doing 'what you can' frees up a lot of the energy absorbed by these often relatively unconscious inner conflicts and is an important part of your response. The other part, which is equally important, is looking after your own wellbeing. The rest of this chapter will focus on this, but before we get there, let's take a quick look at another threat which has much in common with the existential threats we face.

The threat of impermanence

Death. We are all mortal beings. How do you deal with the certainty of your own death, the loss of life itself? Denial can work well in our younger years, but as we age this tends to change. There is a phrase from the wisdom traditions:

"Let death be your advisor."

Being continually mindful of our own mortality can be a powerful motivator for being alive in the moment and making all we can of our lives. If you are concerned, as I am, about the potential collapse of civilisation, there is a sense in which this also is a kind of death. Whilst we know that many other civilisations have been and gone, it seems more frightening when it applies to our own.

It is, I suppose, possible that our present civilisation has to collapse to make way for a better one. I used to think that once global civilisation collapsed, that was the end. Reading Lewis Dartnell's fascinating book, *The Knowledge – How to Rebuild Our World after an Apocalypse*, persuaded me otherwise and gave me hope. However, rebuilding a civilisation is so difficult, and would take so long, that I believe it is much easier to change our present world before it is too late, and avoid the pain of collapse.

But perhaps even the prospect of the collapse of our global civilisation can also be a motivator for seizing the moment and making the best of our opportunities. What I'm pointing to here is the importance of reflecting on the nature of our eco-anxieties and the meanings we attribute to them. The threats may be out there, and we may not have much choice about them, but we do have a choice about what we do with them and what they mean to our personal quality of life. Do we allow them to cause us emotional pain, or can we recover our personal wellbeing in the face of adversity?

In the rest of this chapter I want to focus on personal wellbeing and look at some of the foundations, practices, skills, and qualities that can contribute so much to it.

On personal wellbeing

This chapter explores briefly some of the pathways which offer the greatest promise in the face of our serious headwinds. It's for you to notice which you already use, which are new to you, and which could be worth exploring more.

If personal wellbeing is the aim here, what exactly is it? A thought from Socrates here:

"The good life is a life that questions and thinks about things; it is a life of contemplation, self-examination, and open-minded wondering. The good life is thus an inner life – the life of an enquiring and ever expanding mind."

But first, the predicament at the personal level. Perhaps the majority now believe we are doomed. Surveys show that the levels of anxiety and depression are at an all-time high and rising, especially in children, young people, and indigenous peoples. Rising eco-anxiety is in part responsible and is defined by the American Psychological Society as:

"The chronic fear of environmental cataclysm that comes from observing the seemingly irrevocable impact of climate change and the associated concern for one's future and that of the next generations."

A few more thoughts on this. You've probably heard of the research showing that stronger connections with the natural world can help: going for walks in the natural world, gardening, even growing indoor plants can make a difference.

I'm reminded of the time when I was reading a lot of books on the downsides of our crises. I'd just finished Mark Lynas's Our Final Warning. Grim reading indeed. I went for a walk in the hills with my head full of it. I can still remember the moment when I suddenly became aware of the outrageous beauty of the sunlit landscape; idyllic valleys scattered with little white cottages and the sheep safely grazing. In that moment the world was perfect as it was. And that experience stays with me.

I want next to take a deeper look at personal wellbeing with a quick look at some of the necessary foundations. These foundations are necessary, but not sufficient, which is why we'll go on to a range of skills and practices.

Foundations of wellbeing

This is just a brief checklist to ensure you have all the obvious foundations in place.

Feed your brain well

For your mind to work well, your brain needs to work well, and that means nutrition. Eat mainly plants, as many different kinds as possible, organic where you can afford to, and processed as little as possible. Avoid junk food except as an occasional treat. Most supermarket ultra-processed food is so toxin loaded that human flesh is no longer fit for human consumption.

Not that I'm suggesting…

Get your body working

On exercise, ten minutes a day of aerobic exercise that gets your heart going, your lungs heaving, and that breaks you out in a sweat, is enough to give the toxins in your system a good flushing through and lower your risk of illness. Focus on doing anything you enjoy that gets your heart going.

Sleep well

On sleep, regular habits help. Aim for regular bedtimes. You may not know that sleeping flushes the toxins out of your brain in the same way that exercise does for the body.

Keep learning

Maintain a learning habit. Always be learning something new, preferably across different areas. This stimulates and maintains neural growth in the brain and keeps you mentally fit and young.

Quality friends

The quality of your friendships correlates highly with longer and happier lives. Think here, not of extensive lists of 'friends' on social media networks, but a small group, two to five, of your closest friends. The ones you talk with regularly about whatever matters most in your life. Cultivate these friendships and invest your time in them. They will repay your investment many times over and nourish your soul. If you feel lacking in this area, make it a priority to find and cultivate more close friends.

Meaningful work

Another thing that correlates highly with personal wellbeing is meaningful work, whether paid or voluntary. Surveys show that up to 85% of employees are dissatisfied with their work. If you are one of those, think about changing, if you can, to work that would be more satisfying to you, even if it pays less. Wage slavery isn't fun, and your wellbeing increases in proportion to how meaningful your work is for you. Try to prioritise the quality of your life over your material standard of living. Of course, if life under neoliberal capitalism has not treated you well and you have very low income, or very high expenses, this can be really challenging.

Wellbeing pointers

Here are a few more ideas which you may find helpful. First, what you think about grows! Develop the skill of watching where your attention goes when it wanders, then shift it onto something more nourishing. Reflect on what you feed your mind with. If you focus on the bad news of the world, and the 'news' is mainly bad news, then guess what…

Here's another related idea. Learn to make a strong distinction between what's within your control and what's not. Notice when you are dwelling on matters beyond your control, then switch to thinking about what you can do that is within your control. If nothing, then move on. This is a mental habit worth the effort of nurturing.

One last idea for the moment is this. It's not what happens to you that makes the difference, it's what you do with it; the realms of the inner world again, and challenging. But it is another mental habit well worth cultivating. More on how to do this below under mental rehearsal.

Wellbeing practices

Perhaps the best known and most widely used wellbeing practices are meditation and mindfulness. These practices have developed over thousands of years and are used in many cultures. Initially they are hard work until, with practice, they become easier, but they do work for most people. I will say little of them here except that they give you a way of training your mind to notice your thoughts and feelings in the present moment and be aware of your surroundings. Awareness writ large.

From experience, I think this gives three main benefits. First, you get better at staying in the present moment, a surprisingly difficult skill to achieve as minds naturally wander. Second, you become much more aware of what your mind is actually doing, a non-trivial skill. It's rather like developing a new mental muscle of reflective self-awareness. It tends to shift your identity from being the subject of your thoughts and inner experiences, to being the observer of them. And third, the mind tends to become more still and calm – peace of mind. All three skills tend, with practice, to transfer into the realms of the everyday with an increase in the quality of life; no mean accomplishment and well worth the investment of time and energy.

Hope

Then, of course, there is hope. I cannot overemphasise the importance of hope. Gary Snyder in his book, *The Psychology of Hope*, says the research shows that hope is the best predictor of wellbeing and success in our lives. To have hope, you have to have something to hope for. You also have to be able to imagine a variety of ways of getting there. Finally, you need to find the motivation to take action on getting there. These are skills to be learned, but all three aspects enhance each other, and, like all skills, they become easier with practice.

Snyder's work was one of the inspirations for the approach I've taken throughout this book: hope for a better world, multiple pathways to take towards it, and action steps within your control which you can take to enhance your motivation for your personal journey.

If you would like to boost your levels of hope in the context of the crises we all face, then a useful book is *Active Hope: How to Face the Mess We're in with Unexpected Resilience and Creative Power* by Joanna Macy and Chris Johnstone. They have decades of experience of writing and teaching in this area and cover a wealth of inspirational thinking and practice.

I like the way they frame it as the three stories of our time: business-as-usual, the great unravelling, and the great turning. They then go on to outline the three dimensions of the great turning as: holding actions, life-sustaining systems and practices, and shifts in consciousness.

The domain of the spiritual

A main driver for each of our personal journeys is to be found in the ultimate questions of meaning and purpose, the domain of the spiritual. What are you here for? What is the purpose of your life? What brings meaning for you? Significant questions indeed.

We must each find our own answers to these questions and the answers will change as we make our journey through life. In many of the perennial wisdom traditions, the first part of life is about growing up to adulthood and focussing on family and earning a living; the second part is about spiritual development. As a dear friend of mine put it:

"We must look for the wells that draw on a spirit that leads towards the common good. It is here we discover the springs of hope and the passion and motivation essential for change."

Canon Tim Higgins, Third Order of The Society of Saint Francis

The following exercises are drawn from my experiences over decades of teaching and learning the inner skills of personal development and wellbeing. They can help to clarify purpose, develop wisdom, and enhance the quality of life.

Pathways to wellbeing: personal evolution processes

More now on your inner journey and the pathways to personal wellbeing. Why? Because just as collective wellbeing is the most effective aim for our collective journey, developing your own wellbeing is your part to play in our collective journey. And, as in that question, 'Who cares for the carer?', you have to look after your own wellbeing if you are to be effective in joining with others to address our shared wellbeing.

Any journey has a destination. And for your life to be on track for your wellbeing, you have to have a track to be on. So, what is your track? What is your path, your destination? Also, we all need something to steer by, a compass, and our core values seem to best fit the bill here. What do I mean by core values? Your fundamental beliefs about what's important in life. Only you can clarify these and there are no rights or wrongs. You may already be clear. If so, you would probably be able to list your top five values with little difficulty.

If not, here's a deceptively simple, but not necessarily easy, exercise. I recommend paper, not a screen. The physical act of writing engages different parts of your brain. If you want to go the whole hog, use a dedicated notebook of your choosing.

Core values exercise

The purpose of this exercise is to clarify the internal compass of your top five values by which to better steer your life.

Grab a sheet of paper, or a notebook, and scribble at the top:

'What's important in my life is…'

Now, brainstorm and jot down whatever words, phrases or sentences come up first.

Put each thought on a separate line.

This will give you some clues, but is only the starter.

Notice what you're not happy about, what's missing, or what just feels wrong.

Start afresh and have a second go, then a third, and so on.

Sleep on it and come back to it the following day.

After enough iterations, and it may be ten or twenty, you'll be done.

You're done when your top five values are staying pretty constant.

Hang in there with the process. As I said, it's simple but not easy. This gives you a personal compass to steer by, but a compass is not enough. Your journey needs a destination. Of course this will change over time, but you are here and now, so this is where you start from.

Life purpose exercise

Here the purpose is to explore and clarify what your core life purpose may be. If you think of yourself as being spiritually inclined, this is where matters of ultimate meaning and purpose come in.

Take another sheet of paper, or turn to a new page in your notebook, and write down:

'The purpose of my life is…'

Now brainstorm, and complete the sentence with whatever comes up first.

This will give some clues, but is only the starter.

Notice what you're not happy about in what you've written.

Start a new line and have a second go.

Repeat with a third go, and so on. Sleep on it and come back to it on another next day. After enough iterations, maybe twenty or more, you'll be done. You're done when you have a one-liner life purpose statement which you find motivates you and can help guide your decisions.

When you get to the point of having completed these two exercises, well done! Most people find the processes easier from here on in.

Key life areas

The intention here is to clarify which are currently the most important areas of your life.

On a third piece of paper, or a new page of your notebook, write this question:

'The seven most important areas of my life are...'

You'll be using the same iterative process as for the previous two exercises. If you're curious about why I suggest using this iterative approach, it's because this process encourages an integration of your conscious thinking and your unconscious mind's thinking; this works far more effectively than conscious mind alone.

Life area wellbeing

The purpose of this process is to clarify your level of wellbeing in each of the main areas of your life.

On another page, or a sheet of paper, draw a circle and write down your seven main life areas spaced roughly evenly around the outside.

From each one draw a line to the centre.

For each life area in turn, ask yourself this key question:

'How much wellbeing am I experiencing in this life area?'

Answer this as a number on the scale of 0 = none and 10 = optimal.

Write these numbers on each spoke with 0 at the centre and 10 on the outer edge. You can join them up with a line from one to the next if you wish.

Look at the result and reflect on what it's telling you.

You might want to pay more attention to the areas of lowest wellbeing in the following exercises.

Life intention mapping

The purpose here is to begin mapping your intentions across time. Don't get attached to them; everything is in flux. And bear in mind that life is what happens to you while you're making other plans!

Another page.

At the top left hand write: *'Three Time Frames'*, and just under it, *'Seven Life Areas'*.

Across the top write your three time frames:

'One Week, One Month, One Year' (or whatever your preference).

Down the left column write down your seven life areas spaced out.

In the remaining space, draw a grid of boxes three across and seven down, 21 in all.

In whatever order you are drawn to, reflect on each box in turn, and focussing on this life area and this timeframe, ask yourself these two questions:

'What intention or goal, if I achieved it, would make the greatest difference to my wellbeing?'

'Which issue or problem, if resolved, would make the greatest difference to my wellbeing?'

Fill in each answer as keywords or phrases, taking your best guess at each. They can each be about the same thing, or about different things. Repeat for the other twenty boxes.

As with all the exercises, treat this as lightly as you can. Find ways of making the process engaging and enjoyable. Your answers are not written on tablets of stone and are certainly not intended as a future opportunity to beat yourself up for having failed. They are merely explorations of the unknown; potential steps on your journey.

Daily journalling

The point here is to support your habit of reflective thinking and bringing your intentions into your life. For this, you really do need a dedicated notebook. If you haven't got one, perhaps now is the time to buy one. Perhaps a quick look online for the one you are most drawn to? I use an A5 spiral bound one with unlined pages and keep the pen in the spiral. Choose what suits you. As with all these processes, what works best is tailoring it for yourself. And this is particularly true of the content of your reflective journalling.

However, there are a few keys to getting the most from daily journalling. Find the best time and place for doing it and let this become a habit. Include a few of the intentions and/or issues drawn from your life mapping week (or shortest timeframe). Feed some these into your daily 'to do' lists in your diary. The following day reflect on them. What happened? And what didn't? If something on your 'to do' list doesn't happen, try breaking it down into ever smaller chunks until it does. If it still doesn't happen, keep reflecting on why. You may need to change something.

Use your journalling time as an opportunity to reflect on your life. It doesn't really matter what you write, it's the process of reflecting on your daily life, and what you learn from it, that is important. This is what provides the benefits. However, there are a few aspects of this process which are crucial; these include how you think about your problems and your intentions.

Well-formed issues

The purpose here is to develop useful habits, ways of thinking, about your problems. We commonly get snarled up in how we think about the issues in our lives. Rest assured, this is normal! There are some ways of approaching issues which work better than others. And one of the best is to first clarify what the issue actually is.

Ask yourself:

'What exactly is my problem or issue here?'

Or, if it is just be a feeling of unease about something, ask yourself this:

'What exactly am I uncomfortable about?'

Write down your first thought. This is unlikely to be the real issue, but starts the clarification process. Your aim is to get it down to a one-liner which, for you, hits the nail on the head. Keep repeating this process until you reach the point where it fits the following structure:

Something/anything (a word or a phrase)

causes or means, (makes me; or means that)

some form of emotional pain, (a word or a phrase)

For example:

'My concern about where we're all headed is making me feel anxious and hopeless.'

When you are able to express any problem or issue as this kind of sentence, you've finished this stage and you have a well-formed issue; you've reached the point of diminishing returns. The most useful thing you can do now is to shift your attention to what you want, rather than what you don't want. This is your intention, outcome, goal, or whatever you prefer to call it.

Well-formed intentions

Here, the purpose is to develop productive thinking habits about your goals and intentions. Ask yourself: *'What do I want instead of this problem.'* Make sure the words you use are in the positive, saying what you want, and not in the negative, saying what you don't want.

For example, if your intention is to 'stop worrying about the state of the world', this is mainly a restatement of what you don't want, 'worrying about the state of the world' with the word 'stop' in front of it. On the other hand, 'to feel more at peace with the state of the world' is saying what you want, rather than what you don't want, and is much easier to achieve.

Also, remember to check that the way you word it is in principle within your control, and not under someone else's. For example, your own emotional state is in principle within your control. Someone else's emotional state isn't.

Asking yourself *'If I could have it, would I take it?'*, is really useful for surfacing any objections. These are often in the negative, so flip them into the positive. For example, 'I want to feel more at peace with the world, *but* I don't want to feel powerless'. Flip 'powerless' into what you do want, perhaps 'I want to feel more empowered to do what I can about it.' Finally add this onto your original, 'I want to feel more at peace with the state of the world and to feel more empowered to do what I can about it.' Now repeat the whole process asking, 'If I could have it, would I take it…' until you are congruent, that is, you are free of objections or internal conflicts.

Resolving issues and achieving your goals

The point of this is to use different types of mental strategies to resolve the difference between where you are, the issue, and where you'd rather be, the intention or goal. Usually we try to figure it out with our conscious minds. If that works, fine. But often it doesn't. What then?

One good strategy is to stop trying to resolve it with your conscious mind, and to repeatedly reflect on the difference between where you are and where you'd rather be. This primes your unconscious mind to set to work on resolving the difference. The more you do it, the better it works. At some point you are likely to get an 'Aha' moment when you get a shift, and the problem resolves itself.

The learning question

Here the purpose is to develop more effective internal strategies for learning to resolve issues by changing your own behaviour. The broad gist of it is this. You encounter one of life's problems (again!). You think about the specific situation and ask yourself the learning question:

'What would I do differently next time?'

Then you imagine yourself doing it that way, and repeat until you feel comfortable with it. This avoids the trap of blaming others, which leaves you powerless.

Of course there is more to it than this. For example, if you don't know what to do differently, think who would know, and how they would deal with it. A deeper layer lies behind the question:

'What would I do differently?'

The focus is on doing, which presupposes external behaviour.

The trouble is, all external behaviour comes from the inner world, what you think, what you feel, and what you believe. So the question more usefully becomes:

'How would I need to feel differently, and/or what different assumptions (beliefs) would I need to have, and/or how would I need to think differently? And how would that lead me to act differently in the situation?'

Unwieldy, but effective because it covers all bases.

On feeling differently, ask yourself: *'What other emotional states would work better? When and where have I experienced those?'*

On beliefs, ask yourself:

'What it would be more useful to believe?'

And on thinking differently, ask yourself:

'How could I think about this in a more effective way, or how might someone else think about this more usefully?'

The general principle is to keep on asking yourself better questions. As E. E. Cummings put it:

"Always the beautiful answer who asks the more beautiful question."

So, how can you test out these new thoughts, new feelings, new beliefs, and new behaviours in practice?

Mental rehearsal

The point of mental rehearsal is to build your skills and effectiveness by learning new behaviours. When I worked in organisations, I was surprised to discover that about half of the people had never heard of mental rehearsal and never did it. The other half knew about it and used it quite often, especially whenever they were going into new or challenging situations. They said it was invaluable.

What then is mental rehearsal? It is simply to mentally rehearse any situation to improve how well you deal with it. You imagine the situation in which you want a better result, and you imagine yourself trying out different approaches, a bit like running videos in your mind's eye. As you do this, pay particular attention to the responses of the people you imagine being in the scene with you.

Whenever what you're doing doesn't feel right, stop the video, make some improvement in what you're doing, and run it again. Repeat until you're comfortable with it. Finally, re-run the whole thing a few times until it begins to become habitual. This lays down the new behaviours in your neural networks.

One last piece of fine tuning on this. Most people who use mental rehearsal don't know there are two quite different ways of doing it. When you run videos of yourself in your mind, are you associated, that is, looking out of your own eyes? Or are you disassociated, seeing yourself from outside.

It turns out that the most effective way of doing mental rehearsals is to run them disassociated first, until you are fairly happy with your new approach. Then, you follow that up with running it through fully associated, to fine tune how you are doing what you are doing.

This works because when you are associated you are more in touch with your feelings. When your feelings are amplified like this, you can use them as your guide to fine-tuning the new behaviour.

Notice what happens in the acid test, the real life situation. It either works OK, or it doesn't. And if it doesn't, it's a learning experience, and you repeat the whole mental rehearsal process.

Gradually you build up your repertoire of new skills, both interpersonal and intrapersonal, i.e. with others and within yourself. This becomes a continuous and never-ending process of development and personal evolution.

In summary

The inner skills we've covered here can make a real difference to your wellbeing, especially those of core values, life purpose and the learning question. But if you want to improve your quality of life in any life area or issue, just run it through the personal evolution processes. And do remember, any split between the inner journey and the journey of the outer world is false; both inner and outer are intimately and continuously interwoven.

It may take a while to develop the skills above, but as the combined effect is truly transformational, the investment of a little time is well worth it. Also, as you develop each skill, for example mental rehearsal, it becomes habitual and effortless. Apart from revisiting the first five exercises a few times a year, it all comes down to daily reflective journalling and learning life's lessons as they come up. This only takes ten or so minutes a day.

Enough for now about some of the core skills of the inner journey, central though they may be to the quality of your life. If any of them attract you, try them out and add them to your other inner skills.

Here ends this chapter on the inner journey. In the next chapter, we'll briefly look back at all the different areas we've covered, before looking again at the core dilemma each of us faces: 'Yes, but what am I to do about it all?'

Chapter Twelve
Conclusion: Your Part in Changing Our World

My first readers told me that this book is ideas dense, so I'd like to start with a brief recap of the journey we've made. Then I'll explore the actions we can each take to change things before we run out of time.

Origins

I began by researching a book which I thought would focus on the climate crisis; was there a way through and what would it look like? The topic morphed and grew. Along the way it became clearer that our global systems are locked into a doom loop and that these systems are ultrastable; they are very good at defying all attempts to change them in any significant way.

This led to the quest for something new, an intervention that has the potential power to break us out of the doom loop. As you now know, what transpired was the Citizens' Mandate for Change and the need for a website. What also emerged was the structure of this book, and the urgency of our situation called for a book sooner rather than later. For time is of the essence.

The threats

We have not only looked at the climate crisis, but put it in the wider context of the other main threats we face and the levels of risk involved in each. This included the threats in overshooting our planetary boundaries, the natural risks of asteroid strikes and major volcanic eruptions, and the human-made risks, including nuclear war, pandemics, and dystopian authoritarian rule.

The underlying causes

Starting with surface events and symptoms, we have traced the causes down through a rich picture of our complex global systems to clarify the fundamental underlying causes of our problems. Centre-stage was not human nature, it was the dysfunctional nature of our economic, political and media systems, locked in place by the dominant role of the vested interests of the tiny minority who benefit at an extreme financial scale to the detriment of all.

The Citizens' Mandate for bringing about change

This social and political invention has been spelled out in detail. It is a highly leveraged intervention with the potential to break us out of the doom loop and lead to the emergence of the better world that is possible. We have looked at how, with your support and that of your friends, it could rapidly scale up and hit the social tipping point for change.

Political change

We've thought through some of the different ways this could transform the next election and bring a movement for change into political power with a shared Mandate for Change. These included the possibilities of a transformed Labour Party, of new progressive coalitions, and of the emergence of new parties, including a possible Citizens' Movement for Change party. The key battleground will be at the next general election.

The battle will not be just for different policies, for if the political system stays the same, these new policies will simply be sabotaged by the power of the vested interests. We need to change the political system itself; to rid it of the power of the vested interests. We need nothing less than a new political system, Democracy 2.0 as I called it earlier. Only a redesigned political system can truly give power to the people. And it is necessary to give us the power to redesign the economic system so that it can begin to resolve our problems.

Systems for a world which works

Our main problems stem from the unintended consequences of our economic and political systems and these are systemic problems. The upside of this is that, by changing the dysfunctional systems and by replacing them with systems which are able to do what we want them to, we can resolve most of our main problems. The Citizens' Mandate is the first step in changing these systems.

We looked at what makes systems viable and the Viable Systems Model, one of the most promising approaches to have emerged from the field of systems thinking, and how it has been mapped onto redesigning political and economic systems. The role that exemplars, such as Finland, can play in our transformation is an important one. No less important is understanding how the forces work which are preventing change.

Changing our economic systems

In exploring the economic systems, we've focussed on the dysfunctionalities of the current system of neoliberal economics, before moving on to explore the alternatives. These included the growing field of ecological economics, Kate Raworth's Doughnut Economics model, steady-state economics, and the circular economy.

The changing role of government towards an expanded entrepreneurial state facilitating a GND has been outlined. Then we took an overview of the future role of the business world. This included transforming corporate structures and the new measures, metrics, of carbon productivity and social productivity needed to displace profit-only businesses. This chapter mapped out a synthesis of our best economic alternatives.

The British Green New Deal and Earth for All

Between them, I believe these two policies represent our best options, and they have each been summarised in some depth.

The BGND has the advantage that it has the highest level of public awareness of any feasible options to replace the present way of doing things.

Earth for All, on the other hand, is based on highly trustworthy dynamic computer modelling of Earth systems. The two approaches are broadly making the same proposals and could well be integrated into a best single approach.

Transformation at the national and global levels

In this chapter we examined how transformation could occur as the Mandate spreads and more countries change over to new political and economic systems. A tipping point will be reached when we can look at reorganising governance at the global level.

At the global level, the emphasis was on the development of an effective form of minimal global governance needed to create political and economic systems that work. We looked again at how the transformation can be financially afforded and the kind of timescales needed to implement it.

Thinking in systems for systems that work

As we've seen, since all our biggest problems are fundamentally caused by how our economic and political systems work, or rather don't work, we need to redesign our outdated systems. To do this we will have to make use of the systems thinking science which has been evolving over the last 75 years, but is still not widely known about or used.

This chapter gave a brief introduction to systems thinking before focussing on the work of Donella Meadows and her outline of where to make changes in systems to have the greatest effectiveness. One of the places of greatest leverage is in our mental models and unconscious assumptions. Or, to be more accurate, it is in the mental models of those in power.

The chapter finished with an overview of some of the main branches of applied systems thinking for those who want to, or need to, explore it in more depth. And what a relief it is to know that there are approaches which are able to engage well with the sheer complexity of the mess we are in.

Threats revisited

In looking back at the threats outlined in the first chapter we reviewed the impact that the necessary global transformation would have on each of them. The planetary boundary threats, including the climate crisis, are all massively reduced. We should be able to keep carbon dioxide levels from increasing and even begin to reduce them, so stabilising the climate, and eventually returning it to normal.

Even the natural risks of an asteroid strike can be mitigated to a significant degree, and we may even be able to develop the technology to predict supervolcano eruptions, so minimising the loss of life. The human-made risks of pandemics, nuclear war, and the dystopian threats of authoritarian rule can also be greatly reduced. We will be able to live hopefully again and see huge progress towards a better world for all.

Your inner world

One of the themes that has emerged throughout this book is that it is our inner beliefs and assumptions that tend to glue the systems of the outer world in place. Another theme is the importance of wellbeing as a fundamental goal. Both are significant aspects of our inner worlds of subjective experience.

Unusually for a book of this kind, I have looked at some guidelines and processes for enhancing and developing personal wellbeing. We need to care for ourselves if we are going to look after the wellbeing of others and the world. And last but not least, we come to perhaps the most important question of all. What can each of us can best do about the mess the world is in?

On taking action

There are many options available as responses to our crises. Denial is a common one, and affords some comfort to many. Endlessly complaining about the problems is another popular path, and it may even be therapeutic to a degree. But like denial, it ultimately leads nowhere useful. We can get angry, and there is good reason to be angry, but anger aimed at scapegoats is misguided. However, anger can provide the motivation to do something about it, and doing something about it is better than doing nothing.

Perhaps a combination of concern and anger is what motivates so many of us to join protest movements. This makes a difference, but not enough. Then there is quietly getting on and doing your bit for the environment, or volunteering in so many different ways to address our unmet social needs. Also necessary but not sufficient.

The Citizens' Mandate option

Having your say, by casting your personal Mandate, is arguably the most effective single thing you can do for change. Go to

citizensmandate.com and watch the short video clips to give you the summary the Citizens' Mandate for Change and how it has the potential to change our world before it is too late.

Before submitting your Mandate, we also recommend that you talk it through with friends and family. This serves two purposes. First, it helps you to get clear on what you want to say in your Mandate. Second, it helps to spread the idea. If it spreads it will work. If it doesn't, it won't.

Here, again, are the three key questions of political change for you to think about:

What are the main issues you are concerned about?
What kind of society would you prefer to be living in?
What changes do you want our government to make?

It's well worth visiting the website to get the latest news on how the project is developing. The Mandate option does look promising when added to your other options. As you know, it involves you and some of your friends in meaningful conversations and writing down your answers to just those three questions.

It's low cost and low risk. It's not illegal, indeed it's difficult to see how it could be made illegal. And getting involved in some of the projects which are likely to emerge, of which more shortly, promises to be both personally satisfying and to lead to quality friendships.

A few other plus points. The Mandate is hugely ambitious; no single-issue protests here, we need to change our world systems. You don't have to join anything, there is no membership fee, and no donations as it's all funded by profits from this book.

The Citizens' Mandate is not limited to the UK. You can pass it on to friends abroad and by doing this you are helping to create a powerful international movement. As numbers grow in different countries, they will each develop their own tailored website.

Neither is the Mandate legally limited by age. If someone is old enough to be concerned about their future and the state of the world, then they are old enough to have their opinion heard. Indeed younger people have more reason to speak out.

One of the main benefits of contributing your Mandate is that it lets you have your say and adds to the feeling of doing all you can. The more you believe that it has the potential to change everything, the stronger the feeling of making a difference becomes.

I'm reminded, here, of the 'indulgences' of the Middle Ages. You gave your priest some money, your sins were indulged/forgiven and you could feel OK about them. Is it possible that, in a similar way, by acting on the Mandate you may feel a bit more OK about your carbon sins? A trivial thought perhaps, or perhaps not.

By having the meaningful conversations with your friends which the Mandate involves, you are likely to build deeper relationships with them. And, at the very least, you can add it to the list of things you did in that imaginary conversation with your kids when they grow up and ask you what you did about the climate crisis…

The Citizens' Mandate in other countries

This project has been developed, piloted, and tested in the UK. If the idea is good enough, it will spread to other countries. If you do not live in the UK, what can you do? You can complete the Mandate on this website and tell us which country you live in.

This lets us know when people from your country are interested. We will develop versions of this site for each other country as they get involved. For countries which are not primarily English speaking, I believe we will need translations of the website and this book.

Google Translate could be a big help here. In order to mount a campaign in your country which summarises the results of the Mandate and sends the results to politicians and the media, you'll need help. We need people to volunteer to take this initiative. If you are from somewhere other than the UK, then just get in touch via the website: **citizensmandate.com**

And what else can I do?

Wherever you live, we come back to the central question of what to do. First recognise what you already do and give yourself a pat on the back, and a few karmic credits for good measure. But if you're looking to be more effective, and wondering what that might look like, here's a way of thinking about it which I quite like.

Imagine three overlapping circles, sometimes called a Venn diagram. One of them contains your strengths and skills; what you have to offer. The second contains the most important things you believe need doing in the world. And the third contains things you like doing which bring you joy, satisfaction or wellbeing. Now look to the central area where all three circles overlap and ask yourself this question:

'What do I most love doing which makes my skills and strengths available to this important area of need in the world?'

Ponder, brainstorm, reflect, then go do it.

What can emerge from the Mandate?

As I reflect on the Citizens' Mandate, I'm curious about what may emerge as it begins to grow. We've looked at how it may spread to countries other than the UK, each with their own versions of the website and the book.

Before launching this website or publishing this book, I started to talk with friends about the Citizens' Mandate and noticed that discussion groups started to emerge spontaneously.

In writing this I've tried to pull together some of the most hopeful and promising ideas from leading thinkers and writers across all the fields that seemed relevant. Although I've tried to keep the writing style as light and engaging as possible, the subject matter is necessarily somewhat dense.

It may therefore bear further contemplation and discussion. You might want to re-read one or more chapters to become more familiar with different ways of thinking about our problems. Perhaps study groups will emerge. This book could form a starting point for these. Perhaps there will be demand for an online study group, or a course.

Some may want to give talks about the Mandate to the organisations they belong to or work in. This book and the website can serve as a primer.

Perhaps action groups will emerge, many of which will show up on the website. Some people might want to go door-to-door on their street. You may be able to use the next generation of the Citizens' Mandate website to summarise your neighbours' views and give them a copy of the results. Or you may be able to summarise their views yourself, as one group already has. Those involved are likely to be interested and want to know the results. You could also do this where you work.

It may be that charities, NGOs, businesses, and other forms of organisation will adopt the Mandate to align better with the concerns of their memberships. They may also adapt the Mandate process to slightly different uses as the open question format is potentially powerful and versatile.

Perhaps NGOs and other organisations will use the Citizens' Mandate to build a huge movement of movements; The Citizens' Movement for Change. This could unite so many and would be both hugely empowering and powerful.

With the intended second generation website funded by book sales, we plan to be able to automatically send a monthly summary of constituents' views to MPs. This would certainly get their attention. Some may want to meet with their MP, singly or in small groups, to discuss it.

Summaries by city, county, nation, or the entire UK, could be sent to all politicians and the media. At some point it will be media-worthy, and then it will begin to have real impact.

An online Citizens' Mandate community?

One of the things I'm most hopeful about is the emergence of an active online community. I think this is important so that the Mandate isn't just a one-stop wonder – 'I've done my Mandate, that's it.' We need a way of carrying the conversations forward and building communities for change.

This may emerge on the Citizens' Mandate for Change website, or perhaps on a Citizens' Movement for Change website, or an Alliance for Change website, which combines organisations and citizens for change. Active online communities may emerge on any or all of these. Whatever wants to emerge will. Exciting times!

Only active communities will be able to keep generating the new ideas, the new projects, and the new social activities which will be so essential to achieving success. Either the Citizens' Mandate website, or other websites for change could host online communities for change and will, I hope, give birth to other communities on the main social media sites, as well as to many communities in the real world 'offline'.

I think online communities, as well as local on-the-ground communities, are both essential for expressing these ideas in the wider world and for getting to the key social tipping points. These wider expressions of community and conversations for change are the very processes by which the transformative change happens.

However, as I've said before, these innovations will not be inherently predictable. They are emergent properties of a social system in flux, and they will be self-organising. I think a blend of online and offline communities is the most promising source for these future innovations.

The new ideas will come from community members. The communities acting through their networks will choose the most promising of them. And community members will back the different projects with actions and campaigns with each person choosing the ones they are most drawn to.

Swarmwise, a new form of organising that works

How exactly this may all happen, I don't know. But there are promising models out there. In my view the best I've seen for our purposes is described in Rick Falkvinge's book, *Swarmwise: The Tactical Manual to Changing the World.*

In 2006 he founded the first 'Pirate Party' in Sweden with the intention of getting members elected to parliament. They did get two members elected, but what is particularly interesting is that they succeeded in this with virtually no funding but with the strength of an extensive online community – raw people power. And at their peak they had a Pirate Party in 70 different countries.

They pioneered ways of growing effective, self-organising and non-hierarchical online communities for change. In the book he gives a lot of useful detail on what does, and doesn't, work. I'm usually a little bit on the sceptical side when it comes to the organising abilities of alternative organisations. However, I've read *Swarmwise* three times (there are very few books I've read three times) and will go back to it again as a handbook for action.

If you want to join us and take action, then his is the book to buy. This book is about the theory, while his book is about the practice; they make a powerful combination. You might want to check it out. Swarmwise is a good model to base our movement on.

Some basic principles of the self-evolving organisation

If we are going to create a global phenomenon for political change, we need to avoid the elephant-traps of organising. *Swarmwise* gives us an example of best practice to follow. Here I've tried to distil just a few of the more important ideas and mapped them onto how the Citizens' Mandate based movement for change may evolve.

What is a swarm organisation?

"A swarm organisation is a decentralised, collaborative effort of volunteers that looks like a hierarchical, traditional organisation from the outside. It is built by a small core of people that construct a scaffolding of go-to people, enabling a large number of volunteers to cooperate on a common goal in quantities of people not possible before the net was invented."

Rick Falkvinge

Is there a compelling purpose?

Rick says, your idea needs to be tangible, credible, inclusive, and epic. For a swarm to succeed it needs a compelling vision or purpose. Well, our shared purpose is to change the world for the better before it is too late. Ask big and you get big, as Zack Exley pointed out earlier.

Is there a critical threshold for success?

Yes, 25%, of your friends, 25% of the UK population, and 25% of the global population. As we've seen this is the threshold for social and political transformation.

Are enough people energised by it to pass the critical threshold?

That is what this project will find out. If you find it compelling, then start by passing it on to at least a quarter of your friends. If you want to really get behind it, think about what other ideas and projects you can come up with and make a start. You can also check out what other options there are on the website and get involved with those you find motivating.

How it works

A swarm organisation is open, transparent, and self-evolving. It has shared values, a positive and supportive culture, and a plan. The website and this book map out such a plan. The swarm consists only of relationships between people: perhaps your family, your friends, the people you meet along the way. And a swarm organisation needs a primary task, which in our case is spreading the Citizens' Mandate.

Core facilitators

A swarm needs what Rick calls scaffolding, a framework of core of facilitators, the go-to people whose job it is to support the activity of the other 95% of the swarm.

Their work will include things like developing the website, following and creating social media activity, providing support to projects, looking after financial and legal matters, and dealing with the old media, the press and broadcast media.

Self-organisation

The basic idea of the swarm model is that it organises itself. All we need to do is communicate very clearly what we want to see happen and why we want it to happen.

In our case what we want to see happen is spreading the Mandate to change the world. If people agree, they will make that happen without anyone telling them exactly what to do or how to do it. They will self-organise. People motivated to 'make it so' will gravitate to a subtask where they can help deliver the desired result.

With the Mandate, obviously this includes talking with friends and family, but also starting, or getting involved with, projects. Each person will do this in their own way using their own strengths, with no micro-management or supervision needed.

This is the opposite of the command-and-control model of most organisations, and it is the reason why a self-organising swarm organisation can run rings round any traditional organisation. It can operate at greater speed and scale, but with tiny financial resources.

It is all based on mutual trust by keeping the swarm transparent and giving everybody a very far-reaching mandate to act on their own initiative. A swarm is optimised for three things: speed, scale, and trust.

In practice

Swarm organisations create their own projects and different ways of achieving their main goal. If you have a project, you can just get on and do it. In Rick's Pirate Party, they evolved a few rules of thumb that made this work better.

One was that for any significant project it was wiser to have at least three people agreeing that it was worth trying before going ahead. This is different to having to ask someone's permission and leads to much greater creativity. Another rule of thumb was about seeking the optimum group size for any project or task.

The three magic group sizes

Tight working groups larger than seven tend to fragment. So action groups should aim to stick to this limit. If you are supporting more than seven friends who are spreading the Mandate, it might be better to split them into two different groups for, say, Zoom meetings. This first group size is like a family.

The second group size which the Pirate Party found to be useful in practice is no more than 30 for an activity that involves looser cooperation than a tight working group. This can be thought of as an extended family. It can tackle the tasks that fall between the smallest and biggest group sizes. This might be a door-to-door campaign in a neighbourhood to give people their political voice and get the Mandate out.

The third and largest group size should be 150, known as Dunbar's number after the British anthropologist who first wrote about it.

This limit is followed by many successful organisations. This is our maximum 'tribe' size. Any grouping above this size needs to split. An example for us would be a major campaign across a city or in an MPs constituency.

Swarm projects

In this chapter I've outlined a few possible projects to help kick-start the thinking. One that I've perhaps not emphasised enough is local community action groups. There is much to be said for being able to meet face-to-face with other activists in your area. It really boosts levels of motivation.

As I write, such thoughts are for the future and some of those are for the second generation website, which is intended to be more versatile that the first generation.

Launching the website and book is the first priority. What else may emerge in the future as the project evolves? You will probably have your own ideas...

Individual conversations make the biggest difference

Any movement spreads one conversation at a time, and the starting point of it all is the conversations you have with your friends, family and colleagues. A few thoughts here, and forgive me if these seem obvious.

Only talk with people when it seems appropriate and if they are interested. This tends to happen naturally when related topics crop up. On the other hand, proselytization or preaching at people, is not good. It will inhibit the project, and may well damage your friendships. Respect peoples' views and interest, or lack of it.

Arguing with people is similarly counterproductive, as it tends to entrench their views. However, having discussions based on being respectfully interested in what others believe can be useful and mutually beneficial. Become curious and ask questions like, 'I'm interested, what makes you think that?', 'What led you to believe that?', or 'I'd like to understand why you think that.' Then listen carefully. They will feel heard and are more likely to open up and explore their own thinking. Remember, everyone is right within their own view of the world. And every worldview contains partial truths. We all have much to learn from each other.

Meaningful conversations exploring concerns, ideal worlds, and changes worth making, are enjoyable for their own sake and often strengthen our thinking as well as our relationships. They are the first and most important step to becoming more effective. Indeed, they are perhaps the most important way you can contribute, especially if they lead to more Mandates. Remember, widespread social conversations are the core mechanism by which big transformations happen.

How to have more meaningful conversations

Talking about climate change may sound simple. But most of us don't do it. Instead, we tend to 'self-silence'. As Paul Simon sang, "Silence like a cancer grows." We know it's important, but we can't get the words out of our mouths. According to the research, most people don't talk about climate change. Only a third discuss it even occasionally.

Most of us find it difficult to start conversations about things like the climate crisis or inequality, yet this is how social denial works. Why do we find it so difficult? There are many reasons. It can seem like starting a conversation on politics, religion, sex, or personal finances; it feels uncomfortable. Perhaps we want to avoid making other people feel uncomfortable. Or could it be that we want to avoid becoming uncomfortable ourselves? Why do we not feel OK about it?

Resolving inner conflicts

The climate crisis and the impending collapse of civilisation are the elephant in the room. It affects us all. We tend to experience inner conflict, and this takes a different form for each of us. What form does it take for you? Fear and anxiety are a big part of it for a growing number, but there is also the guilt or shame that comes with knowing that we, and our carbon emissions, are also part of the problem. Or maybe we feel vulnerable and that we will open ourselves to ridicule.

Perhaps you still fly on holidays. This leads to the conflict between the part of you that really wants that holiday and the part of you that feels guilty over flying, knowing the damage it does. It may be similar for fossil-fuelled cars or home heating. Or perhaps meat eating. Only you know the things that you feel torn about and that get to you. What to do about it?

First, recognise the conflict for what it is, parts of your inner self fighting each other. Resist the temptation to deny internal conflict and instead become curious. What are the two sides of this conflict? Recognise that they each have a positive intention. What are they each trying to do for you? Take the example of flying on holiday. Maybe part of you wants to enjoy yourself with a well-earned treat, while another part of you doesn't want to feel bad about the carbon emissions of flying.

What is the positive intention of each part? Maybe one part wants you to enjoy yourself while the other part wants to have a positive impact, rather than a negative one. How else could you do that? Now, as best you can, imagine a future you who has combined the positive intentions of both parts: to enjoy yourself and have a positive impact. Perhaps holidays closer to home?

You may be clear on what combining the positive intention of both parts means and feels like, or it may take time and repeated practice. Either way, this process can resolve the conflict and free up the energy for more useful action.

Who to talk with

Having meaningful conversations is a skill worth mastering. Start by building your confidence with the easiest people and gradually work out from there, learning as you go. The easiest people will be those you have the strongest connections with. They are likely to include close friends and family.

They also include groups you share strong values or interests with. Because of this common ground, you are the best person to talk with them about their concerns, climate change and the Mandate. Your thoughts will carry greater weight with them than with others who don't belong to their group.

Starting a meaningful conversation

There are two different ways of doing this. You can wait for a suitable opportunity to come up naturally, such as someone talking about a closely related subject. Perhaps they are talking about an extreme weather event, then you could ask how much they think it's related to the climate crisis, and go on from there.

Alternatively, you initiate the conversation yourself. You could ask them what they think about climate change. You could disclose that you are concerned about climate change, and then ask them what they think about it. Or you could say you are doing an informal survey on what people think about climate change. Ask them where they are on a scale of 1 to 10 with 1 meaning it's not an important issue and 10 meaning it's the most important issue we face.

You will never find out what people think about climate change unless you ask them. When you do, the research shows that most people are eager to talk.

Either way once they are talking, the next most important step is to listen. Being genuinely curious about their views is the easiest way to listen actively. Listen for whatever seems important to them, and if appropriate, summarise them back, 'So you think that…' or 'So what you're saying is…' This lets them know you are really paying attention and value what they think. Being listened to will make them feel more comfortable talking about it, enabling the conversation to follow a natural flow.

Developing your 'difficult' conversation skills

However, having these conversations go well and feel natural is a skill, and skills need developing. How do you develop your skill in this area? By reviewing each conversation, as soon as possible afterwards. Which bits went well? What was your part in that? What exactly did you say or do? And which bits didn't go so well? What exactly would you say or do differently if you were able to have that conversation again? This, of course, is the skill of mental rehearsal from the previous chapter.

Over repeated conversations with different people, you will gradually become better and more confident, which makes the whole process more enjoyable. The general principles are: listen actively, avoid getting into arguments about climate facts, and focus instead on personal stories about shared values and concerns.

Another important point is not to raise difficult subjects without talking about possible solutions, including things you have done; the Citizens' Mandate fits well here. If you want to know more about all this, Katherine Hayhoe has a few chapters devoted to the topic in her book *Saving Us: A Climate Scientist's Case for Hope and Healing in a Divided World*.

She says, "I do think we are hitting a tipping point in global consciousness. For years I've spoken about the challenge of psychological distance: when people are asked if they are worried about climate change, they say yes; but when asked if it affects them, they say no. That barrier is falling quickly as nearly everyone can now point to someone or somewhere they love that is being affected by wildfire smoke, heating extremes, flooding and more."

She goes on to say, "We have strongly suspected for a while that our projections are underestimating extremes, a suspicion that recent extremes have proven likely to be true."

241

On the importance of conversations, Hayhoe tells the story of an older man, Glyn, who lived in Wandsworth, London, and had watched her TED Talk "The Most Important Thing You Can Do to Fight Climate Change Is Talk About It." This inspired him to have as many conversations as he could. He used the 'how concerned are you' on a 1-10 scale technique. When she met him, he had records of over 12,000 conversations! And all because he had watched one TED Talk about why climate change matters and what we can do about it.

And that wasn't all. His borough had just voted to declare a climate emergency which he believed was because of all the conversations he'd had, including quite a few with key influencers. Two years later they had divested from fossil fuels, invested in renewables, and announced they would be spending £20 million on new environmental and sustainability strategies. An inspiring example; what might you do?

The first step to creating a better future is to imagine it

An important part of having these conversations is to include a better future in them. Everything we humans have created had to be imagined first. This is why it forms the basis of the second question in the Mandate, 'What kind of society would you prefer to be living in?'

So, the first step in creating a new shared future is to imagine it, the imaginary, as some call it. This begins with each of us. When we talk with others about a different and positive future, it develops more social credibility. When this happens at scale, a new social consensus of what is possible emerges. And this of course is what social transformations are, at heart, all about.

Times of crisis are times of opportunity

It is possible that major crises are exactly what it takes to create major transformation. The bigger the crisis, the bigger the opportunity. And just as the crises we face are dire, so the transformations we can create could be the best thing that ever happened, the biggest breakthrough in human history.

There is no law of physics which says that we cannot create a global society better by far than our present imaginations allow. For our imaginations are limited only by our beliefs about what is possible. As the song goes, *"Imagine…"*

It could well be that a far better world awaits us; a world transformed by embedding functional wisdom in the structures and processes of our human organisations and systems. Remember that Gregory Bateson quote:

"The major problems of the world are the result of the difference between how nature works and how people think."

To the extent that this is true, in future the ecology of our human systems may increasingly align with the ecological workings of the natural world to the benefit of both. For Stafford Beer's viable systems are closely aligned with, and modelled on, the workings of the natural world. It is perhaps no coincidence that Beer and Bateson, two intellectual giants of the twentieth century, were friends.

Underpinning both their philosophies, and perhaps that of this book, is a perennial philosophy which integrates the wisdom of the natural world with viable ways of thinking about human society. If this perennial wisdom can be empowered by the 'voice of the people' to break us free of our systemic bonds and the doom loop, there are few limits to what we may achieve in our pursuit of a better world, a veritable eutopia.

Here ends our journey for now. We have explored a path of hope. And it might even be our path of greatest hope. As you finish this book, remember that the end of reading is also the beginning of acting on all you have got from the reading. I will be well pleased if it also adds to the quality of your life and encourages your hope that we can rise to our biggest challenge and create a better world for all.

Closing thoughts

So the real conclusion is to be written by you in your mind, and in your imagination. The fruits will be in your conversations with your friends, and in your actions. They will be witnessed in what you, and they, think, say, and do.

"Today is only one day in all the days that will ever be. But what will happen in all the other days that ever come depend on what you do today."

Ernest Hemingway

Truly, nothing is so powerful as the right idea at the right time. And if it is the right time for the Citizens' Mandate for Change, it really does have the power to change everything. Perhaps little else can.

Live in hope and take action. For together, *we can* change the world.

And we must.

A review by you on Amazon is a small thing that you can do which could make a big difference to the success of this potentially world-changing initiative. Thank you so much for buying the book and supporting the project. John, Sarah, and Mike

Acknowledgements

It takes many people to write a book and the author is but the channel through which it happens. I thank you all. Of course, any errors are mine.

The seeds were sown under the influence of my mentor, Stafford Beer, who I found inspirational. They were nurtured by my teacher Liz Mahoney who believed in the power of possibility and from who I learned so much. And the fertile ground was provided by the thinkers and authors of some thousands of books I have read this lifetime.

I owe a debt of gratitude to my students who have taught me well and to my fellow change professionals in organisational change who have stimulated my creativity and critical thinking.

My special thanks go to Sarah Smith and Mike Leigh who have very actively helped develop the Citizens' Mandate for Change and Global Transformation project over the last few years. Mike has read many of the sourcebooks alongside me and helped to clarify the thinking. He has also spent many more hours meticulously editing the book and creating the Acronyms, Glossary, Bibliography and Index.

My writing mentor, Susan Quilliam has more subtle distinctions in the art of writing than anyone I know and has been unstinting in the generosity of her time and support. She taught me how to write many years ago and supported me in the process of evolving this book.

My long-suffering friends have helped to develop my thinking and many have been first readers of the early drafts. Highly supportive and specific in feedback, I thank you all. You know who you are.

Mike and Sue were not alone in helping with the editing. My thanks go also to Judith van Dijkhuizen, Arthur Musgrave, Martin

Reading, Tim Higgins and Pat Boase. Without this diverse editing, this book could never have become what it is.

My thanks also to Laurence O'Bryan and the good folk at Books Go Social for doing such a good job of the publishing with Amazon Kindle Direct Publishing. Also to Anna Piotrowska at Luz Linea Studios for the lovely cover design.

Last but not least, my dear friend Angela Coleridge has been an unfailing emotional support amidst the many ebbs and flows of the authoring process and the entire project.

I am so grateful to you all for making this work possible.

Appendix 1
Summary of the first Citizens' Mandate results

This was run on a Google forms questionnaire with the results put into an Excel spreadsheet. ChatGPT was then asked to summarise all the answers to each question first as a 60 word summary, then as 20 prioritised bullet points.

The following results came from the first test of the survey software. It is a very small sample of only 23 people and they are all friends of mine, so it is distinctly non-random!

It does, however, successfully demonstrate proof of concept. We can now ask any group of people the three key open questions of change: from what, to what, and how specifically; we can then summarise their collective view objectively and accurately.

This 'qualitative survey technology' is new and has huge potential for good. It has a wide range of applications in many different fields. What other applications can you think of?

As to the content, I find it absolutely fascinating, read on…

First Survey Results for The Citizens' Mandate for Change

This is the Chat GPT summary of all the answers to the first question:

What are the main issues you are concerned about?

Our key concerns for my Member of Parliament encompass a wide spectrum of issues. Foremost is the urgent need to address climate change and its potential catastrophic consequences. Simultaneously, we must reform economic systems to combat growing inequality, secure funding and improvements for vital services like healthcare and education, advocate for a more ethical political system, and ensure social justice, fairness, and environmental sustainability in our society. These multifaceted challenges require immediate and concerted action.

1. Climate change and its potential catastrophic consequences for civilization and global systems.
2. Income and wealth inequality, exacerbated during the COVID-19 pandemic.
3. Slow progress toward achieving net-zero emissions and environmental sustainability.
4. Underfunding of essential state sectors, including healthcare and education.
5. Dysfunctional political and economic systems, lack of democracy, and corrupt lobbying.
6. Growing fragmentation of society, leading to a lack of mutual responsibility, respect, and recognition of non-monetary values.
7. Disrespect towards marginalized groups in society.
8. Affordable housing, poor insulation, and poor air quality contributing to the climate emergency.
9. Tax evasion by the wealthy and the need for fair taxation.
10. The importance of public ownership, co-operative models, and political reforms.
11. The need for a circular economy and reduced extraction of virgin resources.
12. Commitment to the Paris Agreement and transitioning away from fossil fuels.
13. Promoting green energy and biodiversity in national planning.
14. Environmental concerns such as plastic use and nuclear waste.
15. Addressing social justice and inclusivity while reimagining societal structures.
16. Ensuring representation in politics and addressing social, environmental, and economic issues.
17. Subsidizing green initiatives to make sustainability accessible to all.

18. Redirecting government revenue away from fossil fuels and toward green energy incentives.
19. Considerations for taxing excessive profits of oil companies or removing their tax burden if they invest in green energy.
20. Urgent action required to educate and persuade individuals to reduce their carbon footprint to avoid catastrophic global warming.

This is the Chat GPT summary of all the answers to the second question:

What kind of society would you prefer to be living in?

In our ideal society, wisdom, kindness, and respect are paramount, fostering equal access to resources and nurturing individual growth. It's an ecologically conscious utopia, prioritizing well-being and environmental health, promoting regenerative practices, and democratic governance. Education, housing, and healthcare are accessible to all. Social justice, technology for the planet's benefit, and political accountability are vital. This society rejects exploitative capitalism, values relationships, ensures equality, and promotes genuine well-being, all while striving for sustainability and reducing inequality.

1. Our ideal society values wisdom, kindness, and support while providing equal resources to all and promoting commitment to society and individual self-development.
2. It embraces respect for all genders, neurodiversity's, ages, races, colours, and creeds.
3. The society values individuals for who they are, not just for their professions or contributions.
4. Environmental Utopia: It envisions a utopian future where human organizations prioritize well-being and environmental health.

5. This includes addressing pollution, promoting regenerative agriculture, and sustainable food sources.
6. It seeks to allocate half the planet for rewilding and advocates a more participatory and democratic political system.
7. Economic equality is a goal, supporting regenerative businesses and reducing financial disparities.
8. The result is an ecologically sound, high-quality lifestyle for all, fostering a sense of anticipation and human renaissance.
9. Equality and active citizen engagement in shaping the future are central to this ideal society.
10. It strives to eliminate corrosive inequality, encourage hope, and promote inclusivity.
11. Accessible Education and Amenities: Free education, excellent housing, green spaces, affordable public transport, and well-resourced healthcare are priorities.
12. Sustainability and Tolerance: Sustainability, diversity, and tolerance are foundational principles.
13. Negotiation and Mediation: Disagreements are resolved through negotiation and mediation, including the use of Citizens' Juries.
14. Earth Reverence: The society recognises and honours Earth, our sense of belonging, and the sentience of all life.
15. Responsible Technology: Technology is used for benefit without causing harm or enslaving people.
16. Climate Action and Environmental Policies: Climate change is treated as an emergency, lobbying is halted, and environmental support is provided.
17. Taxation and Social Policies: Tax reforms, social justice, universal healthcare, and fair shares are actively developed.
18. Political Accountability: Harsh punishments for lying politicians and tax reforms for environmental sustainability are advocated.

19. Cooperative and Relationship-Centric: Authentic relationships, equality, and respect for people and the environment are key.
20. Public Ownership and Anti-Capitalism: The society promotes public ownership and cooperative models, moving away from capitalism's exploitative nature.

This is the Chat GPT summary of all the answers to the third question:

What changes do you want our government to make?

We want politicians to transform our systems by prioritising lifelong education, healthcare, climate action, and ethical governance. Political reforms, like proportional representation and citizens' assemblies, should foster a democratic system valuing human and environmental well-being. We must transition to regenerative economies, reduce inequality, combat climate change, nurture kindness, strengthen social welfare and healthcare services, all while promoting sustainability. Active citizen engagement and addressing inequalities are crucial to achieving these changes.

1. Prioritize lifelong education, healthcare, climate action, ethics, and kindness in the political system.
2. Shift political and economic systems towards human and environmental wellbeing.
3. Implement proportional representation in the electoral process.
4. Redesign parliamentary systems to involve citizens more in decision-making.
5. Transition to a circular and regenerative economic system.
6. Actively reduce income and wealth inequality.
7. Focus on improving schools in economically deprived areas.
8. Invest in public services and infrastructure.

9. Urgently address climate change and engage in international efforts.
10. Utilize Citizens Assemblies to tackle unresolved issues.
11. Prioritize safeguarding Earth's resources and fostering circular economies.
12. Promote human capital, health, and well-being.
13. Support creative arts and celebrate individual integrity.
14. Implement rituals and ceremonies for reverence.
15. Halt the rise in student debt and invest in vocational routes.
16. Reform healthcare funding and practices for effectiveness.
17. Ensure sustainable energy production and environmental targets.
18. Forge a balanced relationship with the EU.
19. Focus on eco-friendly construction and technologies.
20. Implement policies to combat climate change, tax fairly, and promote healthy lifestyles while preventing undue corporate influence.

Abbreviations and Acronyms

AERPRO – Aerosol Productivity

AGI – Artificial General Intelligence

AI – Artificial Intelligence

B Corporation – A new type of company which is legally obliged to balance a profit motive with the interests of society and the environment.

BGND or **British GND** – British Green New Deal

CAPRO – Carbon Productivity

ChatGPT – Chat Generative Pre-trained Transformer

CRISPR – Clustered Regularly Interspaced Short Palindromic Repeats

Cybersyn – Contraction of Cybernetic Synergy

ET – Extra-Terrestrial

G7 – The Group of Seven

G20 – The Group of Twenty

GND – Green New Deal

GDP – Gross Domestic Product

GNH – Gross National Happiness index

GNP – Gross National Product

HANDY – Human and Nature Dynamics

H5N1 – A subtype of the influenza A virus

IMF – International Monetary Fund

LETS – Local Exchange Trading System

LED – Light-Emitting Diode

MMT – Modern Monetary Theory

NASA – National Aeronautics and Space Administration

NGO – Non-Governmental Organisation

NIPRO – Nitrogen Productivity

PHOPRO – Phosphorous Productivity

PPP – Purchasing Power Parity

SDG – Sustainable Development Goals

SETI – Search for Extra-Terrestrial Intelligence

STV – Single Transferable Vote

SOPRO – Social Productivity

UBI – Universal Basic Income

UBS – Universal Basic Services

VSM – Viable Systems Model

WDP – World Domestic Product

Worgl – An experimental local currency created in Worgl, Austria

Glossary

AERPRO – A measure of the amount of aerosol produced for each unit of carbon used.

Artificial General Intelligence (AGI) – A hypothetical form of artificial intelligence that could learn and solve any problem that human beings can, and more.

Anthropogenic risks – Risks created by human activity, as distinct from natural risks.

B Corporation – A new type of company which is legally obliged to balance a profit motive with the interests of society and the environment.

Biodiversity – The number and variety of living species on Earth. Often used more specifically to the species in one region or ecosystem.

Bretton Woods Agreement – The Agreement that created a global currency exchange regime based on the U.S. dollar and gold and also established the IMF and the World Bank.

British Green New Deal (BGND) – One of the earliest and most comprehensive Green New Deals with a strong international aspect.

Capitalism – Capitalism is an economic system in which the means of production are owned privately or corporately and are used to create profits. This accumulation of capital in the hands of the few leads to them having greater power and influence in changing the system to favour themselves.

Carbon productivity (CAPRO) – A measure of how much of something is produced per unit of carbon used.

Carbon taxes – A tax on fossil fuel use, especially on vehicles, intended to reduce carbon dioxide emissions.

Chat GPT – A language model-based chatbot trained to produce human-like responses and generate essays, articles, poetry and sometimes misinformation.

Circular economy – An economic system, intended to reduce waste and improve sustainability, that is based on the reuse or regeneration of materials or products.

Citizens' Mandate – The normally used abbreviation for The Citizens' Mandate for Change. There are a wide range of other possible types of citizens' mandates.

Citizens' Mandate for Change – This is an innovation, a specific type of citizens' mandate based on the three core questions of change: from what? to what? and how specifically? People answer a version of these three questions and send one copy to their political representative, their MP, and one copy to the Citizens' Mandate website. Here they are pooled and summarised to create a shared political voice. If this invention spreads, it creates a shared political voice at scale. On reaching 25% of the population it has the potential to effect a political transformation.

Citizens' Assembly – A representative group of citizens, selected at random, who are chosen to make a publicly significant decision by choosing expert advisors and using facilitated deliberation.

Citizens' Initiative Review – A small, relatively representative panel that meets to produce a summary for voters on a ballot initiative or referendum to be decided in an upcoming election.

Citizens Income – An income paid weekly, or monthly, to each citizen from their birth until their death.

Citizens' Jury – An alternative name used for a Citizens' Assembly

Club of Rome – A platform of diverse thought leaders who explore complex global issues and suggest solutions to multiple planetary emergencies.

Cognitive dissonance – The mental discomfort that results from holding two conflicting beliefs, values, or attitudes.

Commons – The cultural and natural resources accessible to all members of a society, including natural material such as air, water, and a habitable Earth. These resources are held in common whether owned publicly or privately.

Complexity – Complexity characterises the behaviour of a system or model with many connected parts that can interact in multiple ways, leading to non-linearity, randomness, collective dynamics, hierarchy, and emergence.

Complexity Theory – Complexity theory provides an understanding of how systems, such as the economy and global corporations, grow, adapt, and evolve. It explains how the relationships between members of these systems give rise to the collective behaviour, and sheds light on how a system interacts with its environment.

Consensus reality – Consensus reality refers to the generally agreed-upon version of reality shaped by shared experiences and understandings within a community or society.

CRISPR – Short for 'Clustered Regularly Interspaced Short Palindromic Repeats'. CRISPR is a gene editing technology used for changing genes in any living entity.

Cybernetics – The science of organisation in natural or human-made systems.

Cybersyn – A contraction of cybernetic synergy used for the software and processes used in Stafford Beer's Viable System Model.

Doomsday Clock – The Doomsday Clock is a metaphor for how close humanity is to Armageddon. Since 1947 it has moved from seven minutes to midnight to 90 seconds before midnight in 2023.

Degrowth – Degrowth is a radical economic argument which recognises that we need to put social and environmental concerns before growth of gross domestic product (GDP) as a goal.

Democracy – A system of government based on freedom and equality between people, in which power is held either by elected representatives or directly by the people.

Deliberative democracy – A form of direct democracy where citizens make political decisions through conversation and deliberation about what will best produce the public or common good.

Direct democracy – A form of democracy in which the people themselves decide on policy, unlike a representative democracy where people vote for representatives who then act on their behalf to enact policy.

Doughnut Economics – A visual framework, shaped like a doughnut, of an economy which values human well-being and advocates for a regenerative and distributive economy; it aims to change the goal from endless GDP growth to thriving within planetary boundaries.

Earth for All – An international initiative that offers a pathway to accelerate the systems change needed for a sustainable and equitable future on a finite planet.

Ecological economics – A trans-disciplinary, solutions-based field of studies that recognises the limits of economic growth and focuses on sustainability and development rather than efficiency and growth.

Evolutionary economics – Evolutionary economics is a school of economic thought inspired by evolutionary biology that shuns rational choice theory and points instead to complex psychological factors as key drivers of the economy.

Externalities – In economics, externalities are side effects of an action that don't affect the agent of that action, but instead affect bystanders. Externalities can be positive or negative, depending on their outcome for others, for example, pollution.

Feedback loops – A feedback loop is a cause-and-effect system in which the output of a system feeds back as an input to form a circuit or loop.

Fiscal policy – Fiscal policy aims to guide economic growth, using government spending and tax policies to influence economic conditions.

Free press – A free press supports democracy where it can provide knowledge and information that is not manipulated or serving a particular person, entity or interest. Given that freedom, people can then make the best decisions when they go to vote.

G7 – The G7 or Group of Seven is a political and economic forum for the richest nations to discuss crises affecting the world economy and political issues. Members are the United States, the United Kingdom, Canada, France, Germany, Italy and Japan.

G20 – The G20 is an intergovernmental forum of a group of some 20 countries with some of the world's largest economies including the European Union, that discusses global economic issues such as financial stability, climate change, and sustainable development.

Governance – The processes of governing, whether by a government or an organization.

Gini coefficient – Also known as the Gini Index, it measures the difference between the observed income distribution and a perfectly equal income distribution.

Global currency – A global currency, or world currency, is a currency that would be used by every country for the benefit the world's economy and monetary system.

Green Economy – An economy that improves human well-being and builds social equity while reducing environmental risks and scarcities and aims for sustainable development without degrading the environment.

Green New Deal (GND) – There are a range of different Green New Deal proposals calling for public policy to address climate change along with achieving other social aims, such as job creation and reducing economic inequality. More controversially they often call for continued economic growth.

Gross Domestic Product (GDP) – A measure of the total value of all of the goods made, and services provided, during a specific period of time.

Gross National Happiness (GNH) – This is a measure of economic and moral progress introduced in Bhutan in the 1970s as an alternative to Gross Domestic Product. The "four pillars" of GNH are good governance, sustainable development, preservation and promotion of culture, and environmental conservation.

Groupthink – A psychological phenomenon in which people strive for consensus within a group. The need for consensus can lead to uncritical acceptance of ideas, failure to seek accurate knowledge, or motivation to find creative solutions.

HANDY (Human and Nature Dynamics) – HANDY is a model focussed on the interaction of humans and nature aimed at modelling inequality and the use of resources in the collapse or sustainability of societies.

Information flows – This can refer to the exchange of information among people, processes, and systems within an organization.

International Monetary Fund (IMF) – The IMF is a global organization of 190 member countries. Its purpose is to promote international monetary co-operation, facilitate international trade, foster sustainable economic growth, make resources available to members experiencing balance of payments difficulties, and to prevent and assist with recovery from international financial crises.

Keynesian economics – Named after the influential British economist, John Maynard Keynes, this preceded neoliberal economics in the post-war era. It consists of a number of macroeconomic theories and models referring to how the total spending in the economy strongly influences economic output and inflation.

Legislative Assembly – This refers to a political body which makes legislation.

Limits to Growth – 1972 Report into the probable effects of continued population growth and consumption based on dynamic computer simulations.

Liquid democracy – A form of delegative democracy in which an electorate engages in collective decision making through both direct participation and dynamic representation.

Locked-in – A term from systems thinking referring to the ability of a system to get stuck, or locked-in, to one pattern of behaviour.

Macroeconomics – The branch of economics which deals with the performance and behaviour of an economy as a whole.

Meme – Any pattern of thought and behaviour that is capable of spreading by person-to-person transmission in human societies.

Microeconomics – The branch of economics which studies the behaviour of individuals and companies with respect to the allocation of resources.

Mixed-Market Economy – An economy which contains a mix of private and government services.

Money Creation Committee – A committee which oversees the creation of the money supply of an economy to satisfy the monetary policy.

Modern Monetary Theory (MMT) – A macroeconomic theory which states that a nation that issues and backs its own currency need never go bust.

Monetary policy – A policy adopted by the monetary authority of a nation to affect the supply of money to achieve broader goals such as price stability or high employment.

Nanotechnology – A science and technology based on the study and application of things at the scale of atoms and molecules.

Neoliberalism – The conservative political ideology supporting neoliberal economics.

Neoliberal economics – A type of economics which became the dominant economic ideology of the last 40 years and based on the 19th century ideas of free market capitalism. It favours a small state and policies of privatisation, deregulation, globalisation, austerity, and reductions in government spending.

NIPRO – Nitrogen productivity; the amount of carbon used for each unit of nitrogen produced, mainly in the form of nitrates for fertilisers.

Online democracy – Any form of democratic process which takes place primarily online.

Overton Window – The range of policies that politicians gauge is currently acceptable to the public.

Palma ratio – The ratio of the share of income taken by the top 10% of earners divided by the share of income taken by the bottom 40% of earners.

Paradigm shift – A fundamental change in the basic concepts and practices in any area.

Participatory budgeting – This allows ordinary citizens to participate in deciding on how money is spent on public spending projects.

Path dependence – This refers to any process where past events or decisions constrain later events or decisions.

PHOPRO – Short for phosphorous productivity, this refers to how much the use of phosphorous is productive in terms of how much carbon is used in creating it.

Pragmatism – An approach in which any models or theories are only valued in terms of how well they contribute to the wellbeing of all in practice.

Proportional representation (PR) – Refers to any type of electoral system in which all subgroups of the electorate are represented proportionately in the elected body.

Representative democracy – Also known as indirect democracy, this is the most common form of democracy where elected representatives represent the people, in contrast to direct democracy.

Robin Hood tax – A package of financial transaction taxes proposed by a group of NGOs to be implemented globally, regionally or unilaterally by single countries.

Self-organisation – The ability of a complex system to organise itself.

SETI – refers to the scientific Search for Extra-Terrestrial Intelligence.

Single Transferable Vote (STV) – Sometimes called proportional ranked choice voting, this is an electoral system in which each voter casts a single vote in the form of a ranked choice ballot.

Soft Systems Methodology – A systems approach based on the softer systems of sociology and psychology, rather than the harder disciplines of physics and maths.

SOPRO or **social productivity** – A measure of how much social wellbeing is produced for each unit of carbon consumed.

Sortition – A process of selection by lot that gives all individuals an equal opportunity to hold a position in a citizens' assembly or a government.

Sovereign currency – A currency, a form of money, which is created and maintained by a country which rules itself, a sovereign country.

Steady State Economy – An economy made up of a constant stock of physical wealth (capital) and a constant population size which does not grow over time.

Systems Thinking – A way of thinking about the world as being made up of systems in which parts are in complex relationship with each other.

Supervolcanoes – A supervolcano is the largest type of volcano with an eruption volume of 1,000 cubic kilometres.

Sustainable Development Goals (SDGs) – The United Nation SDGs, or Global Goals, are a collection of 17 objectives designed to serve as a blueprint for peace and prosperity for people and the planet into the future.

Team Syntegrity – A process designed by Stafford Beer usually involving 30 people divided into 12 overlapping teams to deal with broad and initially ill-defined issues.

Tipping point – A threshold which, if exceeded, leads to a major behaviour change in the system in focus.

Tobin Tax – A proposed tax levied on spot conversions of one currency to another to slow down currency speculation, and increasingly applied to all forms of short term transactions.

United Nations (UN) – An intergovernmental organisation whose purposes are to achieve international cooperation, and maintain international peace and security.

Universal Basic Income (UBI) – A guaranteed set income paid by government instead of benefits to all individuals regardless of their means, circumstances, or contribution.

Universal Basic Services (UBS) – Provision by government of certain basic public services according to need. These public services could include, for example, housing, transport, childcare and adult social care.

Viable Systems Model (VSM) – A framework developed by Stafford Beer for thinking about, understanding, diagnosing, and working with complex organisations.

Wellbeing – Used in this book in the sense of a flourishing wellbeing as in the little used terms eudemonia and eudemonic.

Wellbeing Corporation – A corporation whose main purpose is to improve the wellbeing of all people it touches, and the natural world.

World Bank – The World Bank is an international financial institution that provides loans and grants for capital projects to the governments of low and middle-income countries.

World Economic Forum (WEF) – An International non-governmental organisation for public-private sector collaboration known mainly for its annual meeting at Davos in January. It is funded by its 1,000 member companies with turnovers in excess of US$5 billion.

World Happiness Report – A publication with articles and reports on international self-reported happiness rankings.

World Health Organisation – (WHO) A specialised agency of the United Nations responsible for international public health.

World Trade Organisation – (WTO) An intergovernmental organisation that regulates and facilitates international trade.

Bibliography

Introduction

Hawken, P., *Blessed Unrest,* Penguin Books, 2008 – p6
Covers the scale of the global movement for change.

Dixson-Decleve, S, and others, *Earth for All: A Survival Guide for Humanity*, New Society Publishers, 2022 – p17
A project to resolve the climate crisis and inequality well-grounded in computer simulations.

Meadows, D.H., *The Limits to Growth*, Universe Books, 1972 – p17
Classic book which challenged the primacy of economic growth with computer simulations.

Hawken, P., *Drawdown: The Most Comprehensive Plan Ever Proposed to Reverse Global Warming*, Penguin, 2018 – p22
200 experts outline 100 of the best projects to reduce atmospheric carbon dioxide.

Falkvinge, R., *Swarmwise: The Tactical Manual to Changing the World*, CreateSpace Independent Publishing Platform, 2013 – p26
Founder of The Pirate Party outlines how to create big and effective movements for change.

Chapter One

Lynas, M., *Our Final Warning, Six Degrees of Climate Emergency*, Fourth Estate, 2021 – p30

Outlines the likely effects of each degree of climate warming up to six degrees above normal.

Klein, N., *This Changes Everything,* Penguin, 2015 – p30
How our present economic system is damaging life on earth and the need to replace it with something radically different.

Ord, T., *The Precipice – Existential Risks and the Future of Humanity,* Bloomsbury Publishing, 2021 – p42
Looks at the main risks endangering the future of humanity.

Orwell, G., *1984,* William Collins, (Collins Classics) 2021 – p47
Classic outline of a totalitarian surveillance state.

Thunberg, G., *The Climate Book,* Allen Lane, 2022 – p30
Greta's experience plus the knowledge of climate experts on what we need to do to resolve climate change.

Well, H.G., *The War of the Worlds,* Alma Classics, 2017 – p49
A fictional account of how human civilization had to face its possible end.

Chapter Two

Graeber, D. and Wengrow, D., *The Dawn of Everything – A New History of Humanity,* Penguin, 2022 – p51
Revisits the dawn of humanity in light of recent archaeological and anthropological finds highlighting our cooperative nature.

Willis, R., *Too Hot to Handle,* Bristol University Press, 2020 – p56
The inside story of why politicians behave as they do with regard to the climate crisis.

Chapter Three

Blackmore, S., *The Meme Machine*, Oxford University Press, 2000 – p66
A profound summary of meme theory and how far it goes to explain human behaviour.

Bond, B. and Exley, Z., *Rules for Revolutionaries – How Big Organising Can Change Everything*, Chelsea Green Publishing, 2016 – p75
What works in organising at scale for change, based on the Bernie Sanders campaign.

Centola, D., *Change: How to Make Big Things Happen*, John Murray, 2022 – p79
How big change happens, how ideas spread and are adopted, and how movements grow.

Dawkins, R., *The Selfish Gene*, Oxford University Press, 40th Anniversary edition, – 2016 – p66
The book that first introduced the idea of a meme as a self-replicating behaviour.

Gladwell, M., *The Tipping Point: How Little Things can make a Big Difference*, Abacus, 2002 – p79
Explores examples of how tipping points work.

Chapter Four

Alexander, J., *Citizens*, Cadbury Press, 2022 – p108
Thinking of ourselves as citizens rather than consumers and embracing citizen power.

Arriaga, M., *Rebooting Democracy: A Citizen's Guide to Reinventing Politics*, Lucius & Lamb Publishers, 2014 – p96
A global journey exploring examples of doing democracy better.

Bouricius, G.T., *Democracy Through Multi-Body Sortition: Athenian Lessons for the Modern Day*, Journal of Public Deliberation, Volume 9 Issue 1, April 2013 – p104
Outlines a way of running a more democratic parliament base on citizens' assemblies.

Chomsky, N., *Profit Over People*, Seven Stories Press, 1999 – p85
A damning critique of neoliberalism.

Dunt, I., *How Westminster Works… and Why It Doesn't*, W&N, 2023 – p92
Description of what has gone wrong with British Government and a version of how we can fix it.

Keynes, J.M., *The General Theory of Employment, Interest and Money* (1936), Wordsworth Editions, 2017 – p84
Keynes reconsideration of classical economics that changed economic thought and government economic policies.

Monbiot, G., *How Did We Get into this Mess?*, Verso Books, 2023 – p85
A critique of the current mess we're in and the current consensus that got us here.

Stiglitz, J.E., - *Globalization and Its Discontents Revisited: Anti-Globalization in the Era of Trump*, Penguin, 2017 – p 85
A critique of the problems of globalisation for the USA, Europe, and the Global South.

Van Reybrouck, D., *Against Elections: The Case for Democracy*, Bodley Head, 2016 – p104
The case for replacing representative democracy with one based on citizens' assemblies.

Wilkinson, R and Pickett, K., *The Spirit Level: Why Equality is Better for Everyone*, Penguin, 2010 – p85
Classic work summarising the research showing financial equality works better for all.

Wolf, M., *The Crisis of Democratic Capitalism*, Allen Lane, 2023 – p99
Makes the case for democratic capitalism based on the separation of wealth from power.

Chapter Five

Beer, S., *Platform for Change*, John Wiley & Sons, 1975 reprinted 1995 – p116
Presents Beer's argument for change and includes a summary of the Viable Systems Model.

Beer, S., *Designing Freedom*, Garden City Press, 1974 – p116
A brief introduction to cybernetics and how it can help an ailing society.

Dorling, D., and Koljonen, A., *Finntopia - What we can Learn for the World's Happiest Country*, Agenda Publishing, 2020 – p123
An exploration of how Finland, an international top scorer, does so many things so well.

Piketty, T., *Capital in the Twenty-First Century*, Harvard University Press, 2017 – p123

Examines how the political economy of the free market produces wealth and inequality.

Weiner, N., *Cybernetics or Control and Communication in the Animal and the Machine*, Mockingbird Press, 2023 – p115
The theoretical foundations for the multidisciplinary field of cybernetics that influenced so many disciplines including: systems thinking, complexity theory game theory, psychology, sociology, and organizational theory.

Chapter Six

Chandler, D., *Free and Equal: What Would A Fairer Society Look Like?* Allen Lane, 2023 – p146
Expands on John Rawls' thought experiment on designing an ideal society.

Cooperrider, D, and Selian, A., *The Business of Building a Better World*, Berrett-Koehler Publishers, 2021 – p151
A visionary look at the future of business by 29 scholars and executives.

Daly, H., *Steady-State Economics: Second Edition with New Essays*, Island Press, 1991 – p140
An update version of Daly's pioneering classic work exploring the notion of steady-state economics.

Hardin, G., (1968) *The Tragedy of the Commons*, Science 1234 – p131
The original work outlining how commons can fail through overexploitation.

Jackson, A. and Dyson, B., *Modernising Money: Why Our Monetary System Is Broken and How It Can Be Fixed*, Positive Money, 2013 – p142
Private banks create 97% of all money; replacing this could solve many economic problems.

Kelton, S., *The Deficit Myth*, John Murray, 2020 – p145
Outlines how Modern Monetary Theory can pay for all the changes society needs.

Laloux, F., *Re-Inventing Organisations: A Guide to Creating Organisations Inspired by the Next Stage in Human Consciousness*, Nelson Parker, 2014 – p156
Describes an enlightened organizational model that could be needed to collaborate towards changing our future world.

Le Flufy, P., *Building Tomorrow – Averting Economic Crisis with a New Economic System*, First Light Books, 2023 – p152
Describes a new economic system and how we can help build it to avoid the potential catastrophe of our present system.

Lietaer, B. and Dunne, J., *Rethinking Money: How New Currencies Turn Scarcity Into Prosperity*, Berrett-Koehler Publishers; Illustrated edition, 2013 – p157
Rethinks the concept of money and seeks to demystify our competitive economic system with its cycles of financial meltdowns.

Mazzucato, M., *Public Purpose: Industrial Policy's Comeback and Government's Role in Shared Prosperity*, Boston Review, 2021 – p148
With chapters by 23 authors covering an industrial policy agenda for new national goals.

Mazzucato, M., *Mission Economy: A Moonshot Guide to Changing Capitalism*, Penguin Books, 2021 – p148

Explores the new roles governments must take if we are to overcome our collective problems.

Ostrom, E., *Governing the Commons*, Cambridge University Press, 1990 – p132
Key work laying out how to solve the tragedy of the commons by collective action.

Raworth, K., *Doughnut Economics*, Random House Business, 2018 – p137
This hugely influential book introducing the doughnut economy is classic innovative thinking on the new purpose of the economy for a truly sustainable future.

Smith, A., *The Wealth of Nations*, 1776, Various editions since 1776 – p139
First outline of how the invisible hand of the market can turn self-interest into common good.

Standing, G., *Plunder of the Commons - A Manifesto for Sharing Public Wealth*, Pelican, 2019 – p132
Covers the history of the commons and a proposed charter for commoning in the future.

Stoknes, P.E., *Tomorrow's Economy: A Guide to Creating Healthy Green Growth*, The MIT Press, 2021 – p161
Tools for healthy growth by transforming government practice and individual behaviour.

Chapter Seven

Dixson-Decleve, S, and others., *Earth for All: A Survival Guide for Humanity*, New Society Publishers, 2022 – p185
A project to resolve the climate crisis and inequality well-grounded in computer simulations.

Kuhn, T.S., *The Structure of Scientific Revolutions*, University of Chicago Press, 50th Anniversary Edition, 2012 – p172
A formative text on how paradigms change in science which laid the basis for how we now think of paradigm shifts.

Meadows, D.H., *The Limits to Growth*, Universe Books, 1972 – p185
Classic book which challenged the primacy of economic growth with computer simulations.

Pettifor, A., *The Case for the Green New Deal*, Verso, 2019 – p170
One of the developers of the Green New Deal outlines the case for it.

Webster, K., *The Circular Economy: A Wealth of Flows*, Ellen MacArthur Foundation, 2017 – p171
Overview of the emerging model of circular flows for a prosperous and sustainable economy.

Chapter Eight

Lovelock, J., *Gaia Hypothesis*, Oxford University Press, 1979 – p205
Lovelock's original hypothesis that life on Earth self-regulates the conditions for life.

Schumacher, E. F., *Small Is Beautiful*, Vintage, 1993 – p198

Written 50 years ago, 'Small is Beautiful' made the revolutionary case for building our economies around the needs of communities, rather than corporations.

Chapter Nine

Bateson, N., *Small Arcs of Larger Circles*, Triarchy Press, 2010 – p225
Moves systems thinking on a generation with new concepts of symmathesy and vitae.

Bateson, G., *Steps to an Ecology of Mind,* University of Chicago Press, 2000 – p225
First published in 1972 this classic work by one of our most creative thinkers covers patterns in cybernetics, anthropology, psychiatry and epistemology.

Bateson, G., *Mind and Nature,* Hampton Press, 2002 – p225
Written in 1978, Bateson does no less than provide a new way of thinking about the world around us. We must, he says, learn to 'think as Nature thinks,' if we are to learn to live in harmony on the planet.

Beer, S., *Beyond Dispute: The Invention of Team Syntegrity*, John Wiley & Sons, 1994 – p222
A more democratic and effective way of team talking and thinking in organisations.

Boulton, J, Allen, P, and Bowman, C., *Embracing Complexity – Strategic Perspectives for an Age of Turbulence*, Oxford University Press, 2015 – p 224

Explores the profound sub-discipline of systems thinking, complexity theory and practice.

Checkland, P., *Soft Systems Methodology in Action*, John Wiley & Sons, 1999 – p223
One of the first sub-disciplines of systems thinking to focus on the soft skills of enquiry.

Jackson, M.C., *Critical Systems Thinking and the Management of Complexity*, Wiley 2019 – p225
Comprehensive overview of the different branches of systems thinking in theory and practice.

Meadows, D.H., *The Global Citizen*, Island Press, 1991 – p213
A compilation of Meadow's articles on systems thinking for the lay reader.

Meadows, D.H., *Thinking in Systems,* Chelsea Green Publishing Co, 2017 – p213
A classic introduction to basic systems thinking.

Seddon, J., *The Whitehall Effect*, Triarchy Press, 2014 – p223
A damning account, from a systems view, of how Whitehall has failed our public services.

Senge, P., *The Fifth Discipline*, Century Business, 1990 – p223
Branch of systems thinking focussing on the behavioural patterns of systems as described as archetypes.

Chapter Ten

Graeber, D., *Bullshit Jobs: The Rise of Pointless Work, and What We Can Do About It*, Penguin, 2019 – p241
An anthropologist's examination of the spread of meaningless work and the harm it causes.

Hawken, P., *Drawdown: The Most Comprehensive Plan Ever Proposed to Reverse Global Warming*, Penguin, 2018 – p233
200 experts outline 100 of the best projects to reduce atmospheric carbon dioxide.

Monbiot, G., *Regenesis: Feeding the World Without Devouring the Planet*, Penguin, 2022 – p230
Vision of a new future for food and humanity based on advances in soil ecology.

Wilson, E.O., *Half-Earth: Our Planet's Fight for Life*, Liveright, 2017 – p231
A project to conserve half the land and sea to safeguard the biodiversity of our planet.

Chapter Eleven

Dartnell, L., *The Knowledge – How to Rebuild Our World after an Apocalypse*, Vintage 2015 – p225
Explores basic technologies for rebuilding civilisation after collapse.

Macy, J. and Johnstone, C., *Active Hope: How to Face the Mess We're in with Unexpected Resilience and Creative Power*, – p261

Snyder, G., *The Psychology of Hope*, Free Press, 2010 – p260
A classic book on the psychology of hope as a learnable skill.

Watzlawick, P., *The Invented Reality*, W.W. Norton, 1980 – p251
Examines how 'realities' are constructed rather than discovered and
how, once discovered, they are then assumed to be 'real'.

Chapter Twelve

Falkvinge, R., *Swarmwise: The Tactical Manual to Changing the World*,
CreateSpace Independent Publishing Platform, 2013 – p291
Founder of The Pirate Party outlines how to create big and effective
movements for change.

Hayhoe, K., *Saving Us: A Climate Scientist's Case for Hope and Healing in
a Divided World*, One Signal Publishers, 2022 – p303
Shows how shows how many small conversations about the
environment can produce big results.

Index

Printed in Great Britain
by Amazon

42989089R00165